In *Preaching to Connect Truth to Life*, Dr. Benji Kelley gives us a crash course in preaching. He offers an in-depth analysis of the history of preaching and then gives clear and practical insight into how to communicate the Bible in a way that connects today.

—**Craig Groeschel**, founding pastor of Lifechurch.tv and
best-selling author of *It, The Christian Atheist*, and *Weird*

This book provides fresh insights for preaching by examining sermon structure and style from the perspective of the hearer. If you are ready to take your preaching to higher levels of faithfulness to the biblical narrative, relevancy for today, and deeper impact for the gospel, you need Benji Kelley's *Preaching to Connect Truth to Life*.

—**Mark Batterson**, lead pastor of National Community Church and
New York Times best-selling author of *The Circle Maker*

Every seven days! It's the rhythm of the primary communicator. And if it's true that the "pulpit drives the church," then Benji Kelley's *Preaching to Connect Truth to Life* is high octane fuel for the preacher. Using the Bible to illuminate, Pastor Benji dynamically sifts the various styles to challenge how we deliver truth and grace! If you want to elevate the art of preaching, read and reflect.

—**Kevin Myers**, founding senior pastor of 12Stone Church

With a commitment to biblical truth and a desire to engage people in the twenty-first century, pastor Benji Kelley delivers this important book for those wanting to be more effective preachers of the gospel. In a day when the church needs pastors to not only communicate but connect, this work is timely and extremely helpful.

—**John C. Maxwell**, pastor, speaker, and best-selling author

More than a "how to" book, this is a WHY book! *Preaching to Connect Truth to Life* is a one-of-a-kind, brief, compelling journey through the history of preaching. It speaks to the impact of three different styles of preaching: expositional, topical, and narrative. Benji articulately blends them all together, adding the dimension of contexualization, with current examples of life transforming results! The prophet Amos described our current age as "not a famine of food or a thirst for water, but a famine of hearing the words of the LORD" (Amos 8:11). This book offers a powerful answer to that famine!

—**Jo Anne Ly**~ ~~~~~~~ ~~~~~~~~~ ~~~~~ yan Church

D1306496

Finally, a book on preaching that offers a solid historical analysis of the homiletical landscape, while at the same time guiding preachers in proclaiming a fresh Word in the twenty-first century! *Preaching to Connect Truth to Life* is a balanced, thoughtful, and incredibly helpful guide to faithfully preaching the gospel message of Jesus. Buy it, read it, and apply it—you will not be disappointed!
—**Dale Galloway**, pastor, author, and founder of Beeson Institute for Church Leadership

This is a must-read book because its author is a must-hear communicator. His preaching style is one reason why thousands have come to the church he leads. *Preaching to Connect Truth to Life* shows the elements he's drawn from the three major approaches to preaching and how readers can follow a similar path to improve their own style.
—**Warren Bird**, coauthor of *Better Together*

Preaching to Connect Truth to Life equips the reader to imaginatively and effectively interact with the biblical text for the ultimate advancement of the gospel and glory of Jesus. I highly recommend this book without reservation.
—**Jim Garlow**, senior pastor of Skyline Wesleyan Church

Dr. Benji Kelley is one of the freshest voices in the country when it comes to effectively proclaiming God's timeless Word in the twenty-first century. Kelley masterfully demonstrates how to weave the old with the new, while never compromising the truth of God's Word. If you desire to more effectively and relevantly communicate the Bible, while at the same time holding fast to the truth of the gospel, than this is a must-read book for you!
—**Wayne Schmidt**, vice president, Wesley Seminary at Indiana Wesleyan University

Preaching to Connect Truth to Life is a must-read for all biblical communicators. Benji Kelley has done a superb job in combining both a scholarly and practical approach to preaching for changed lives. He's a great communicator himself and now delivers insights for all who aspire to improve their teaching gifts. I highly recommend and enthusiastically endorse this book!
—**Dan Reiland**, executive pastor, 12Stone Church and author of *Amplified Leadership*

Benji Kelley's personal journey to develop as a preacher is inspirational and instructive for all pastors. He outlines the strengths and weaknesses of various styles and then illustrates one style that can be effective in reaching the postmodern world. This is a book I will recommend to all of my pastors.
—**Steve Babby**, district superintendent,
Pacific Southwest District, The Wesleyan Church

Benji Kelly does an excellent job of connecting the historical moorings of preaching to the present challenge of contextualizing the gospel in the twenty-first century. His emphasis on the narrative as a common thread to compliment other preaching styles provides a strong framework for effective communication. Any pastor or student desiring a foundation for their preaching will gain significant value from reading this book.

—**Phil Stevenson**, director of church multiplication and
leadership development, Pacific-Southwest District, The Wesleyan Church

A hallmark of Benji Kelley's preaching is that he consistently and intentionally gives God the glory. And God blesses Pastor Benji with an unusual anointing. What he shares in this book will bless those who love God and the Word. Enjoy this book on preaching from a man who loves to preach and does it extremely well!

—**Dan Leroy**, district superintendent of North Carolina East Wesleyan Church

This book is a must-read for those who wish to better communicate the gospel of Christ to postmodern listeners in life changing ways.

—**Ernest Mullins**, assistant district superintendent of
NC East Wesleyan Church and director of Evangelism and Church Growth

Dr. Benji Kelley is a gifted communicator who has developed the ability to reach multiple generations of people due to his unique communication style. His secrets to effective preaching and reaching the current generations with the truth of Scripture are revealed in this book. I highly recommend it.

—**Craig Dunn**, CEO, Wesleyan Investment Foundation

preaching to connect truth to life

the power of narrative to tell the story

Benji Kelley

wesleyan
publishing
house

Indianapolis, Indiana

Copyright © 2012 by Benji Kelley
Published by Wesleyan Publishing House
Indianapolis, Indiana 46250
Printed in the United States of America
ISBN: 978-0-89827-528-5

Library of Congress Cataloging-in-Publication Data

Kelley, Benjamin.
  Preaching to connect truth to life : the power of narrative to tell the story /
Benjamin Kelley.
      p. cm.
  Includes bibliographical references (p.).
  ISBN 978-0-89827-528-5
1. Narrative preaching. 2. Preaching. I. Title.
  BV4235.S76K45 2012
  251--dc23
                        2012004975

All Scripture quotations, unless otherwise indicated, are taken from the
HOLY BIBLE, NEW INTERNATIONAL VERSION®. Copyright © 1973, 1978, 1984
by the International Bible Society. Used by permission of Zondervan. All
rights reserved.

Scripture quotations marked (ESV) are from The Holy Bible, English Standard
Version® (ESV®), copyright © 2001 by Crossway, a publishing ministry of
Good News Publishers. Used by permission. All rights reserved.

Scripture quotations marked (MSG) are taken from The Message. Copyright ©
1993, 1994, 1995, 1996, 2000, 2001, 2002. Used by permission of NavPress
Publishing Group.

Scripture quotations marked (NASB) are taken from the New American Standard
Bible®, Copyright © 1960, 1962, 1963, 1968, 1971, 1972, 1973, 1975, 1977,
1995 by The Lockman Foundation. Used by permission.

All rights reserved. No part of this publication may be reproduced, stored in
a retrieval system, or transmitted in any form or by any means—electronic,
mechanical, photocopy, recording or any other—except for brief quotations
in printed reviews, without the prior written permission of the publisher.

To my beloved wife Amy Lynn and our five children—
Anna Grace, Benjamin Cole, Wesley Jacob,
Caleb Timothy, and Joshua Hunter. All of you inspire
me with the sermons you live. I love you.

36065700284541

contents

foreword

When the Beeson Pastor Program of Asbury Theological Seminary visited 12Stone in 2001 for a leadership conversation, I found a kindred kingdom spirit in Benji Kelley. He possessed a soul fire for Jesus that burned for spiritually unresolved people. From that day forward our hearts were knit.

As Benji spoke of God's call to plant a church in Chapel Hill, North Carolina, we traded "what if's" that seemed ignited by God's Spirit. And that is the story of new**hope** church.

Benji's love for spiritually lost people is rivaled only by his love for the people he pastors. This set the stage for an amazing core group that would help launch a church of over six hundred on their grand opening Sunday in 2002.

Up close, I have been able to see the workings of a spiritual leader who navigates audacious faith and effective ministry. Tough leadership calls and calling his people to reach higher, they opened their first campus on thirty-six acres of land in the heart of central North Carolina.

Most recently, new**hope** church launched an aggressive multi-site ministry with six campuses, and the passion to reach people for Jesus multiplied again.

If this is what God can do through Benji, Amy Lynn, and the people of new**hope** in just ten years, then it's just a platform for what God has in store. Recognized by *Outreach* Magazine as one of the fastest growing churches in America for the past two years, leading over one thousand people to Christ in 2011, and celebrating their tenth anniversary as they push into five thousand people a weekend is among the reasons other leaders and communicators would want to follow the ministry of Benji Kelley and invest time in this book.

I am so grateful for the early days of pouring into Benji until it birthed a friendship that has led to Harley Davidson rides and kingdom envisioning. I believe you'll be better equipped for communicating the gospel because Benji gave himself to write *Preaching to Connect Truth to Life*. I hope you will get all you can from this book.

KEVIN MYERS
founder, senior pastor, 12Stone Church

acknowledgements

I have always wondered what I would say in the acknowledgements of my first book. There are so many people who have played a significant role in my life. However, for the sake of space, I will broad stroke my comments of appreciation when possible, and specifically identify those who have meant so much.

I want to thank those people through whom God has so richly blessed my life. Simply put, you know who you are, and without your love, encouragement, and support, any attempt on my part to write a book on a subject of such importance as preaching God's Word would indeed be intolerably inadequate and unacceptable to say the least. There are hundreds of you from both Carolinas at various churches. I am thankful to all of you for pouring into me as a young believer, pastor, and preacher of the Word!

More specifically, I want to begin with those who have taught me so much with regards to teaching and preaching the Word of the Lord. I am extremely grateful for Drs. Richard Lischer, William Willimon, William Turner, Elsworth Kalas, and Dale Galloway. Your practical experience in ministry on display in the academy and your belief in God's ministry through me has profoundly changed my life and encouraged me to follow more faithfully in the footsteps of the preacher from Nazareth, Jesus Christ.

I am eternally grateful to pastors Phil Jones, Sterne Bolte, Mark Yoder, and Steve Shugart. Among you and through you in my home state of South Carolina, God began to stir within my heart the calling to which I will now spend the rest of my life in passionate pursuit and gratitude. Not only have you affirmed me outwardly and supported me spiritually, you have also loved me unconditionally and therein enabled me to love and understand myself as one of God's children, called to proclaim the good news of Jesus Christ.

I would like to thank Charlie Dunn of the Docent Research Group, who played an integral role in bringing this book to life! His original, insightful, and creative work played a vital role in helping me transform my doctoral dissertation into the book that is before you.

A special thanks to the church family of new**hope**. You make ministry the thrill of my life. I appreciate your enthusiastic support of this writing endeavor. I know I am biased, but you are the most beautiful local church on the face of the planet. You are nothing less than a joy to serve.

I would be remiss if I did not express my heartfelt thanks to my beloved wife, soul mate, and partner in life, parenting, and ministry: Amy Lynn. Your love and steadfast commitment to Jesus and his church encourages me daily as I fulfill my calling as a preacher of the gospel. Your willingness to follow God's call upon our lives, while being the most unbelievable mother to our children is more than any man deserves. You are, by far, the most precious person in my life, and because of you, I am a better pastor, dad, scholar, and hopefully the husband you deserve. Thank you for seventeen wonderful years of marriage and friendship and five beautiful children that resemble your gifts and graces.

Lastly, I want to thank my children: Anna Grace, Benjamin Cole, Wesley Jacob, Caleb Timothy, and Joshua Hunter. Absolutely nothing in life brings me happiness and fulfillment like being your dad and you being my children. I will spend all the days of my life trying to be the best dad I can be for you, while also encouraging you to follow Jesus all the days of yours.

Without all of you and the love of Christ, any attempt on my part to write a book would be fortuitous, if not impossible. No words can adequately express my deep appreciation for the ways in which you have shown me the eternal importance of the local church. I ask that you accept the following prayer as a simple thank you, a scriptural prayer that asks you to continue in the work of God's kingdom, which you have started and shared so well!

"May the God of endurance and encouragement grant you to live in such harmony with one another, in accord with Christ Jesus, that together you may with one voice glorify the God and Father of our Lord Jesus Christ" (Rom. 15:5–6 ESV).

introduction

The New Testament books of 1 and 2 Timothy give the modern reader insight into the apostle Paul's heartbeat for developing young, pastoral leaders like Timothy who would carry the mantle of preaching the gospel long after Paul was gone. In 2 Timothy 2:15, Paul wrote, "Do your best to present yourself to God as one approved, a workman who does not need to be ashamed and who correctly handles the word of truth."

The problem in a postmodern, twenty-first-century context is trying to decipher what Paul meant when he instructed Timothy to handle the truth correctly. Is there more than one way to proclaim that truth? Was Paul advocating for one particular method or style of preaching that, if employed, ensures a faithful and effective proclamation of biblical truth? Is there a particular way of communicating the truth so that it pierces through the various and sundry worldviews and assumptions that comprise our current culture? Is there a style of preaching that most effectively edifies the body of Christ and actually develops fully devoted followers of Jesus? All of these are valid and necessary questions!

Over the years, these questions and more have been summarized into one, overarching question about preaching style and which of the three dominant styles of preaching—expository, narrative, or topical—is most faithful and effective in the twenty-first century. That is the central question before us.

Through his book, *As One Without Authority*, Fred Craddock instigated something of a "Copernican Revolution" in modern preaching.[1] The most noticeable change was in the preacher's turn toward the hearer. Before Craddock, preachers primarily focused on the authority of the Word of God and their responsibility to deliver the Word in its purest form. For most, this was reflected in what we know today as expository preaching, the style of preaching that continuously directs the attention of the hearers back to a single Bible passage through verse-by-verse explanation.

But with Craddock's leading, newer, seemingly uncharted styles of preaching began to develop. These newer styles turned the task of preaching more toward the hearer. Two of the results of this turn are what we know today as narrative preaching and topical preaching. However, as we will soon discover, variations of these new styles have existed from days of old. It turns out, Solomon was right when he declared, "There is nothing new under the sun" (Eccl. 1:9).

Like the expository preacher, most narrative and topical preachers also consent to the authority of God's Word, but they deliver the Word in a totally different fashion. Unfortunately, the growth of these two newer styles of preaching has led to a predicament in which proponents of one style of preaching have often felt compelled to criticize one or more of the styles of preaching that they do not personally use. The expository preacher may critique narrative and topical preachers for telling cute stories and pandering to the needs of the hearer. The narrative preacher may assume the expository preacher is an extreme fundamentalist and the topical preacher only interested in satisfying contemporary needs at the expense of faithfulness to the biblical text. The topical preacher may insist that the expository preacher is living in a distant and archaic world of three points of irrelevancy and a poem, while the narrative preacher is so obsessed with the biblical narrative that the needs of the people are neglected. In the crossfire, the question of how to most faithfully and effectively communicate God's truth to modern audiences goes relatively unanswered, buried under a burning heap of criticism.

The task before us, as men and women called by God to preach the Word, is to navigate these troubled waters to identify the most effective and faithful way to preach the gospel in our contemporary context. We will look in-depth at this preaching predicament that arises when preachers and professors analyze and evaluate the three predominant preaching styles. We will carefully examine the history of the three styles of preaching, noting the strengths and weaknesses of each. We will learn from the data analysis of a sermon research team. And as a result, we will arrive on the other side of these troubled waters with a better understanding of the most effective and faithful way of proclaiming the one and only gospel we so deeply treasure.

Before we can offer suggestions and solutions, we must closely consider the nuances of the preaching predicament at hand. In order to make any headway in navigating this predicament, we must also examine the current climate of pluralism so rampant in our culture and churches today. These stylistic differences and our culture's outright disdain for truth make proclaiming the gospel an incredibly difficult task. There is hope, though, and this is a journey worth taking together. I am thankful you are along for the ride and trust that the journey will encourage, equip, and inspire you to more effectively and faithfully preach the Word of the Lord!

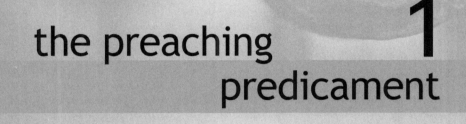

the preaching
predicament

1

I am personally and intimately acquainted with the preaching predicament that most communicators of the gospel experience from time to time—this choice between expository, narrative, and topical preaching—and I have often felt conflicted by it. Living in three different geographic locations in my lifetime has certainly not appeased my inner conflict, since each location provided an opportunity to be exposed to and influenced by a different style of preaching.

In my hometown of Sumter, South Carolina, I was primarily exposed to and shaped by expository preaching. After coming to faith in Jesus Christ at the age of eighteen on October 23, 1988, I was taught the Word of the Lord by two senior pastors, Phil Jones and Sterne Bolte, and my good friend and youth pastor, Mark Yoder. All three men of God were proud advocates of the expository style of teaching. In fact, I was actually discipled in a one-on-one setting by my youth pastor who modeled this verse-by-verse style of teaching Scripture. In time, I was hired as a youth pastor in a nearby church and, as might be expected, I taught and discipled the students within my ministry in the same verse-by-verse expository fashion.

Three years later, while acquiring two master's degrees at Duke University's Divinity School in Durham, North Carolina, I learned the more contemporary, narrative style of preaching. For six years, I walked the hallowed halls of this academy, coming under the teaching and tutelage of some of the best narrative preachers and professors from around the world. As a result of these influences (and my desire to pass the preaching courses), my preaching took a dramatic turn in the direction of narrative.

Finally, while pursuing my doctoral studies in the Beeson Pastor Program at Asbury Theological Seminary just outside of Lexington, Kentucky, I traveled with twenty-two other Beeson pastors to study the largest, most effective churches in the world. As a result, I was introduced and exposed for the first time to the topical style of preaching the Bible. To be honest, there were times when I felt like screaming, "Enough already!" As soon as I would start to grasp the intricacies and disciplines of crafting one particular style of message, my ministry and educational setting would thrust me into an entirely new style of preaching and the learning process would start all over again. Needless to say, my ministry contexts and training have been interesting and confusing, but never dull.

This conflict of styles was never as evident for me as it was during my time at Asbury Theological Seminary (1999–2000) when I joined a professor and twenty-two Beeson pastors from around the globe to dialogue about biblical preaching. Most communicators of the gospel want to be biblical preachers, and that was surely the case in this discussion. Nevertheless, strikingly clear was the fact that many of us differed in our styles and concerns as to what constituted biblical preaching. Repeatedly, the differing nuances of personal preference ricocheted between competing styles of expository, topical, and narrative preaching until it finally reached a feverish pitch.

The tension in the room was palpable and finally exploded with our professor raising his voice in clear frustration to declare, "Regardless of which preaching style you use, you better make sure you preach the text or you will fail this course!" It was an intense moment, but in the end it did nothing to bring about resolution, and in fact, it further exposed the tension I had been experiencing for close to a decade. Though it sounds right to say, "Preach the text," it does absolutely nothing to help decipher the differences between the three styles, nor does it help the preacher know which style is most effective and faithful to the Word of God. Proponents of all three preaching styles believe themselves to be preaching the text. As I walked home that crisp fall afternoon, the confusing and conflicting tension between these three preaching styles was still present and stronger than ever. I had to probe deeper.

In years following, as I prepared to start new**hope** church in the Raleigh, Durham, Chapel Hill, and surrounding areas in North Carolina, I knew that I still needed to settle this issue in my own spirit. While I hope never to settle completely into only one style of preaching, I do believe there is a direct correlation between my preaching style and the effectiveness of new**hope** church's vision to reach, teach, and release. I believe the same can be said of any preacher. If indeed "faith comes from hearing, and hearing through the word of Christ" (Rom. 10:17 ESV), then this is a subject of utmost importance.

Having identified the preaching predicament that most gospel communicators have experienced at one point or another, it is imperative that we identify and probe beneath the surface of the radical culture of relativism that is so prevalent in our postmodern world. If we do not rightly understand the tricky context in which we live and within which we have been called to ministry, then regardless of our preaching style, we will not have a chance of standing up to the Enemy and his schemes.

the importance
of truth in a
relativistic society

2

Truthiness is defined as "what one wishes to be the truth regardless of the facts." That was the American Dialect Society's 2005 word of the year.[1] Unfortunately, that word is also indicative of our current, cultural perspective on truth, authority, and, generally speaking, any sort of governing standard.

In his book, *Radically Unchurched*, Dr. Alvin Reid explains that there has been a gradual decline of morale in youth generations leading to the present. He says the 1940s youth generation lost hope with the experience of World War II. The 1950s youth generation lost innocence with the entry of television into society. The 1960s generation lost the importance of and reverence for authority figures as political and social institutions were increasingly challenged by various entities. For the 1970s youth generation, the idea of love was demeaned as life suddenly became all about me and my individual preferences and desires. In the 1980s, a loss of hope again reared its ugly head with the seemingly overnight proliferation of AIDS and other sexually transmitted diseases. The 1990s youth generation then lost a sense of safety, with the widespread experience of drugs and school shootings. Reid goes on to say, "It's no wonder that by the 2000s we have a youth generation which has almost totally lost any concept of truth and a governing standard."[2]

We see it in the media's disdain for any one truth, yet a love for all manner of personalized opinions, op-eds, and "spiritualities." We see it in the actions of prominent institutions like the *New York Times*, which after learning that author James Frey's 2003 best-selling book about his life as a drug addict, *A Million Little Pieces*, was largely fabricated, still continued to publish it on their Bestseller Paperback Nonfiction List.[3]

Even Christianity has been influenced by a relativistic idea of truth. In answering an interviewer who asked whether Jesus was wrong when he said that he was "the way and the truth and the life" (John 14:6), Cardinal Francis Arinze, a then possible successor to Pope John Paul II, responded:

If a person were to push what you said a little further and say that if you're not a Christian you're not going to heaven, we'd regard that person as a fundamentalist . . . and theologically wrong. I met in Pakistan a Muslim. He had a wonderful concept of the Koran. We were like two twins that had known one another from birth. And I was in admiration of this man's wisdom. I think that man will go to heaven. There was a Buddhist in Kyoto, in Japan. This man, a good man, open, listening, humble—I was amazed. I listened to his words of wisdom and said to myself, "The grace of God is working in this man." The interviewer then repeated the question, "So you can still get to heaven without accepting Jesus?" "Expressly, yes," stated Cardinal Arinze.[4]

The reality is that in our society and the postmodern context in which we live, truth is invented or created out of thin air. Moreover, your truth is not better than my truth and most people, oddly enough, are perfectly at peace with the tension of two diametrically opposing truths. In our relativistic culture of truthiness, as leading postmodernists like Richard Rorty have stated, "Truth is made rather than found."[5]

The problem with this relativistic perspective on truth is twofold. First, it demeans the ability of God's Word to inform and transform our lives from the selfish and self-centered states in which we all live and which serves as the basis of all conflict in the world. Second, it leaves people, Christians and non-Christians alike, even more broken and shattered when the pains of life hit and they have nothing to lean on but a few opinions, platitudes, or bookmark-esque proverbs they once read in the local bookstore.

demeaning God's Word:
"my God is like . . . ?"

Author and theologian A. W. Tozer wrote, "What comes into our minds when we think about God is the most important thing about us. . . . The most portentous fact about any man is not what he at a given time may say or do, but what he in his deep heart conceives God to be like. . . . I believe there is scarcely an error in doctrine or a failure in applying Christian ethics that cannot be traced finally to imperfect and ignoble thoughts about God."[6]

Incidentally, Tozer's sentiment was not original with him. He drew it from the apostle Paul, who stated two thousand years earlier, "Do not be conformed to this world, but be transformed by the renewal of your mind" (Rom. 12:2 ESV). Both men understood something fundamental to our lives: What we think about God determines how we live, for better or worse. This means that unless we have an objective standard by which to govern our thoughts about the divine (Scripture), then we run the risk of living according to subjective and erroneous notions about God, the results of which can be spiritually dangerous!

For example, if we wrongly think that God does not exist, we will not see a need to conform our lives to any divine rule. We can live as we please, however morally or immorally we choose. The character Ivan Fyodor Karamazov, of Fyodor Dostoyevsky's novel *The Brothers Karamazov*, illustrates the idea that if there is no God, everything is permitted.[7] Karamazov's character evidences a philosophy that everything becomes lawful when, in people's minds, there is no god or idea of immortality. The spiritual and practical implications of such a philosophy of irreligion are obvious—a life lived without regard to God or others.

It is not only irreligious concepts of God that are rooted in error. Religious concepts can also be erroneous. For example, if we mistakenly view God as a genie, granting those who pray three wishes, then we need only to make sure that we ask for the right things at the right times . . . nothing more and nothing less.

However, if we have a standard like the Bible that informs our conceptions and perceptions of God, then we see that he not only exists, but that he, as the Creator of the universe, has a particular and wonderful plan for our lives; specifically, one which involves worshiping and enjoying him in the midst of a community of believers known as the church, who daily participate in the redemption of the world's brokenness. Such truth changes everything with respect to how we think and live. It is all contingent upon having a standard-bearer of truth, as opposed to a conglomeration of relativistic opinions about God and the world around us, which will ultimately lead us to demean our Creator. Moreover, when the storms of life come, and they will come, we will not find ourselves struggling with how to incorporate disconnected "truths" into a religion or spirituality that is unfortunately grounded in shifting sand (Matt. 7:24–29).

shattered lives: "what now?"

One of the success stories of new**hope** has to do with a woman by the name of Teresa Mitchell Rad. Teresa came to our church one Sunday morning as a result of taking a Sunday morning drive and noticing a new**hope** church street sign with blue and yellow balloons attached. At that time in her life, she had already consumed large amounts of this Kool-Aid of relativism and was fully convinced that all ways led to God. Educated at the University of North Carolina, she had a keen mind that had been thoroughly submersed in the liberal education of our day. Teresa and I became friends and would often discuss matters of politics, religion, and faith. Teresa was the quintessential poster child for embracing a kind of radical pluralism; she believed wholeheartedly that my truth was no better than her truth and vice versa.

Over the course of a five-year friendship, I was privileged to see God truly get a hold of Teresa's mind, heart, and life. In time, she fully embraced the gospel of Jesus being the way, the truth, and the life (John 14:6), and was baptized as a believer! Later, she even hosted small groups and served on the leadership team that put together the plans and executed our first capital campaign. Teresa was a brilliant marketer who led the way in terms of marketing new**hope** church. That was before she was diagnosed with stage 3 lung cancer.

After experiencing a severe cold that led to pneumonia in March 2009, Teresa found herself in the hospital hearing those dreadful words that none of us ever want to hear. Over the course of the next nine months, we talked, cried, prayed, and discussed the difference Jesus had made in her life. From time to time, we would reflect on how empty and hollow this trial would have been if she had not come to authentic faith grounded in the Bible. Teresa's heartbreaking and unfortunate story ended on a glorious note as she passed from this world into the next. As a community of faith, we wept together at this dreadful disease, yet we celebrated the hope of the gospel and the eternal life that Teresa enjoys in Christ. On December 7, 2009, with her three young boys trying to make sense of it all, our church had its first funeral service in the building Teresa had helped publicize to the community at large.

There are many more Teresas still left to reach for Jesus in your community and mine. As preachers, how do we step into this conundrum of relativity with even a chance of standing up against the Enemy and his schemes? The answer, I believe, is related to how effectively and faithfully we preach the truth of the gospel. If we are going to be both faithful to the Bible and effectively loving toward those who are dying without Jesus, we must try to identify those styles or elements that give us the greatest chance of reaching people with the amazing grace of Jesus.

Is there a style that lends itself to faithfully engage the challenging and pluralistic culture in which we live? Is there a homiletical element that, when integrated into any style of preaching, grants the preacher a hearing and thus a greater possibility of converts surrendering to the authority of the Bible and the lordship of Jesus? As you will soon see, I truly believe there is an element that can greatly increase our preaching potential. Lest I rush ahead and offer some suggestions and potential solutions prematurely, let us first survey the historical landscape of the three most dominant styles of preaching: expository, topical, and narrative. In doing so, we will be able to identify and incorporate various strengths from each style into our proclamation of the gospel.

a brief history of   3
preaching: expository,
topical, and narrative

Anyone who has spent significant time in the great state of North Carolina knows that there are a few key ingredients that make up the cultural landscape here, ingredients that are as much a part of the DNA of a North Carolina native as stripes on a zebra. They are, in no particular order: a zeal for college basketball that rivals that of warring, indigenous, tribal factions; an ability to consume such unhealthy amounts of sweet tea that Lipton comprises the majority of one's arterial system; and the knowledge that beneath the top layer of all North Carolinian terra firma lies an impenetrable layer of concrete-esque soil known as red clay. We North Carolinians believe that the "red" in the name is not only a description of its appearance, but also indicative of its hellish origins. The problem with this "soil of Satan" is that it is deceptive. It appears like a rust-colored sand and therefore seems easily dealt with until you begin digging that post hole or planting that azalea bush and you realize that digging it up is about as easy as skateboarding uphill on gravel. However, good stuff can grow out of the clay so long as you have the right tools.

The same goes for preaching. All good preachers want their sermons to grow "good gospel stuff" in the hearts, minds, and lives of their hearers. Yet before preachers will see growth from their labor, they must take into account the historical preaching landscape. It seems that God never fully reveals himself to any one generation. As such, it is wise for us to survey the historical landscape of expository, topical, and narrative preaching. In doing so, we are given the necessary tools to till that landscape, if you will, and more effectively scatter the seeds of God's Word in the lives of his people (Matt. 13:8–9).

The primary purpose of the Christian preacher is to proclaim Jesus Christ and his crucifiction and resurrection from the dead. Just as innumerable roads of Rome bound the Iron Empire together, and ultimately converged on the City of Seven Hills, all faithful Christian preaching culminates and converges on the primary purpose of pointing people to the life, death, and resurrection of Jesus. Just as the various Roman roads took different pathways, so do the various and nuanced ways in which men and women preach the gospel. Is one particular style of preaching Christ most effective and faithful? Does God's Word favor one particular style of sermon? This is rightfully up for debate. However, before we can even begin such a discussion, we must first understand the most popular preaching styles in the history of the church.

three prominent preaching styles

The three major changes in preaching history can be equated with the harvesting of three different crops: expository, topical, and narrative preaching. At specific times in history there have been marked shifts in preaching around these three styles.

Dr. Robert Smith, professor of divinity and Christian preaching at Beeson Seminary says that the preacher is simply to be an exegetical escort, walking the listener into the throne room of God by drawing attention to the cross, not disregarding theology and not diminishing grace and then leaving him there so that God can do his work.[1] I love that definition of preaching because it masterfully communicates an affirmation of all styles of preaching, so long as those styles both affirm the power of the articulated Scripture with its focus on the gospel and communicate that Scripture in a winsome, rhetorical way. It is a definition that evidences both biblical faithfulness and effectiveness in communication, no matter if your stylistic preference is expository, topical, or narrative. It is also a definition that is representative of the varied and rich heritage of preaching throughout church history.

the biblical period

If we start in the beginning of the Bible and read it through the lens of proclamation, the first noticeable sermon style we find is exposition. James F. Stitzinger, associate professor of historical theology at The Master's Seminary, writes regarding the Old Testament "preachers": "Those originally charged with the task of proclaiming God's Word revealed God to man as they spoke. This Word from God came through different instruments, including the prophet who spoke a divine word from the Lord, the priest who spoke the law, and the sage who offered wise counsel (Jer. 18:18). The [Old Testament] is replete with the utterances of these revelatory preachers who accurately explained God's message to men."[2]

Stitzinger asserts that these original proclaimers of God's Word, like Moses speaking to Israel in Deuteronomy 31–33, or Joshua giving his farewell address in Joshua 23:2–16 and 24:2–27, were strictly expository speakers because they sought to explain to their countrymen the message given them by God. It could easily be argued, however, that they and other biblical figures at times spoke with narrative and topical styles. After all, John Broadus pointed to the "finely rhetorical use of historical narrative, animated dialogue, and imaginative and passionate appeal,"[3] elements that were certainly not exclusive to expository preaching, but were used by these biblical figures nonetheless. Stitzinger also says,

"Perhaps the greatest examples of [Old Testament] preaching are found among the prophets. . . . Prophetic messages were not only predictions of the future (Isa. 9, 53), but often called the people to repentance and obedience (Isa. 1:2–31) or offered the people an explanation of the Word of the Lord (Isa. 6)."[4]

Though many of these prophecies were expository in nature, many others, like Jeremiah's Lamentations and David's Psalms, incorporated narrative elements, invoking, for example, the narrative history of Israel as God's people to eloquently weave the promises and precepts of God into the story of the children of God.

As we transition from the Old Testament to the New, we come upon the greatest preacher who ever lived—Jesus Christ, "who is both the model of preaching and the message preached."[5] Jesus came on a mission of preaching (Mark 1:14) and teaching (Matt. 9:35), but lest we mistakenly put him in a particular preaching box, it is important to note that his "style" was probably best characterized as a style not defined by any one style. On the one hand, Jesus preached expository sermons like those of the Sermon on the Mount (Matt. 5–7) and the one at Nazareth (Luke 4:16–30).[6] With such sermons, he instructed and enlightened his audience by explaining the ancient Jewish texts with great authority and power, as Mark 1:22 says.

However, at other times Jesus preached in parables, which as Lenny Luchetti says, "did not always tie up loose ends in the name of practical relevance. Jesus' parables were structured by a narrative, not linear, logic."[7] In other words, Jesus made as much use of narrative elements in his preaching and teaching as he did of expository elements.

Furthermore, it could also be said, that Jesus' Sermon on the Mount, which is considered by many to be the quintessential expository sermon, was also topical in many respects. After all, the sermon itself begins not with a particular passage of the Old Testament needing to be explained, but rather with the topic of true blessing and the statement: "Blessed are the poor in spirit, for theirs is the kingdom of heaven" (Matt. 5:3).

Moving through the New Testament, we find the preaching of the apostles and other early church leaders. Stitzinger rightly asserts, "The messages of Peter (Acts 2:14–36), Stephen (Acts 7:2–53), Paul (Acts 17:16–31), and James (Acts 15:14–21) have elements of both revelatory and explanatory preaching. The epistles are, for the most part, written expositions designed to teach various [topical] lessons."[8] Like Jesus, the apostles also employed various styles of preaching.

the early Christian church, a.d. 100–476

After the resurrection of Christ and the passing of the disciples, a marked shift in the style of Christian preaching occurred: a turn from preaching the "pure" Word. In its place, we find a new focus pertaining to the "art of the sermon" that was more about rhetoric and style than mere explanation of truth.[9] It was the result of "the fusion of the biblical necessity of teaching with the Greek notion of rhetoric."[10] It was not only about what was said in the sermon, but how it was said. The result was that sermon style quickly became even more varied between the expository, topical, and narrative styles. Even the apostolic fathers (around A.D. 96–125) began to follow a typological method of interpretation in their works. Second-century fathers (around A.D. 125–190) such as Justin Martyr and Tertian composed apologies in defense of Christianity. And third-century fathers (around A.D. 190–250) such as Cyprian and Origen were polemicists, arguing against false doctrine.[11]

By the fourth century (around A.D. 325–460) and the close of the early Christian church era, expository preaching again took center stage. Notable preachers like Basil, Gregory of Nazianzen, Gregory of Nyssa, Augustine, John Chrysostom, and Ambrose each elevated a concern for simply explaining and applying the Bible to daily life. No doubt, the early church period displayed a variety of preaching styles.

the medieval period, a.d. 476–1500

The dawn of the medieval period only contributed to the growing diversity in preaching styles. While the close of the fourth century was a high point for the expository style, the beginning of the fifth through the fourteenth centuries was a high point for the topical style. The reason was the influence of the scholastic theology of the universities and their combined curriculum of theology, philosophy, and the application of Aristotelian logic to the interpretation of Scripture.[12]

Even though the period produced some famous preachers such as Peter the Hermit, Bernard of Clairvaux, and Thomas Aquinas, none would rightly be characterized as exegetical teachers.[13] However, they were neither biblically unfaithful nor culturally ineffective in their efforts at communication.

As the medieval period drew to a close, several pre-Reformation teachers of God's Word arose who did possess a more expository bent to their preaching and teaching. Among these was John Wycliffe (1330–1384), William Tyndale (1494–1536), John Huss (1373–1415), and Girolamo Savonarola (1452–1498).[14] With the contributions of these teachers, along with those like Clairvaux and Aquinas who had come before, it continued to become clear that the advancement of God's kingdom through the preaching and teaching of his Word would not be strictly limited to any one style.

the reformation period, a.d. 1500–1648

With the arrival of the Reformation, the history of preaching styles would shift yet again. Given that the Reformation was built on a foundation of questioning certain church practices, traditions, and sacraments through the lens of the Bible, it became natural for proponents like Martin Luther and Ulrich Zwingli to preach in a more expository fashion. This style was demonstrated by leaders like John Calvin (1509–1564), who said in the first edition of his *Institutes*, "The minister's whole task is limited to the ministry of God's Word, their whole wisdom to the knowledge of his Word; their whole eloquence, to its proclamation."[15]

To people like Luther, Zwingli, Calvin, and later contemporaries, including Henry Bullinger (1504–1575) and John Knox (1513–1572), expository preaching was absolutely necessary given the Roman Catholic abandonment of the Bible in the formation of its doctrines, traditions, and practices.

the modern period, a.d. 1649–present

Succeeding the Reformation era and its leaders were the Puritans, a class of preachers and teachers also known for a staunchly expository style. Contemporary preacher D. Martyn Lloyd-Jones stated that to the Puritans, "true preaching is the exposition of the Word of God. It is not a mere exposition of the dogma or the teaching of the church. . . . Preaching, they said, is the exposition of the Word of God; and therefore it must control everything."[16]

But as effective as the Puritan expository style was in faithfully and relevantly communicating God's Word, it would not be the only style of the modern era to be used by God. Rather, the Puritan era quickly gave way to the Evangelical Awakening, which was divided into the First and Second Great Awakenings. The preaching of this era was led by evangelists like John Wesley and George Whitefield, and was generally topical in nature.[17] Yet, it was this topical style of preaching that had such a profound impact on daily religious life in America, that Benjamin Franklin once said, "From being thoughtless or indifferent about religion, it seem'd as if all the world were growing religious, so that one could not walk thro' the town without hearing psalms sung in different families of every street."[18]

Throughout the rest of the later nineteenth and twentieth centuries, preaching would continue to vary, mainly between expository and narrative styles. Prominent expositors in both Britain and America included John A. Broadus (1827–1895), John C. Ryle (1816–1900), Alexander Maclaren (1826–1910), Charles Haddon Spurgeon (1834–1892), Harry Allan Ironside (1876–1951), Donald Grey Barnhouse (1895–1960), George Campbell Morgan (1863–1945), D. Martyn Lloyd-Jones

(1899–1981), John R. W. Stott (1921–2011) and presently John MacArthur, Jr.[19] Parallel to these expositors, however, were homileticians, like Fred Craddock, William Willimon, Barbara Brown Taylor, and Eugene Lowry, who have been modeling and fiercely advocating for a more narrative sermon style for the last three decades.

Obviously, this is not an exhaustive perusal of the history of preaching. But when you briefly survey the historical and biblical landscape of Christian preaching, it is easy to see that one size does not fit all. In fact, it seems that over the years God delights in using various and sundry preaching styles to communicate the saving grace of Jesus. As such, for those called to the ministry of the Word, it only makes sense that we do our best to understand the three most prominent styles of Christian preaching and how they might enhance our sermons and the communities we serve. To that task, we now turn.

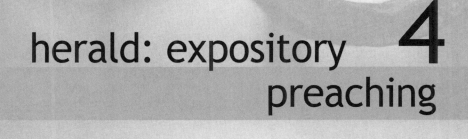

herald: expository preaching

4

In chapter 3, we looked at a brief history of preaching and the various shifts in style that have occurred over the course of that history. Throughout the remainder of this book, we will narrow the scope and drop down from a thirty-thousand-foot level to more of a ten-foot level so that we can observe and analyze the intricacies and nuances of each style and how they have played out not only in history, but in the Bible itself. The hope is that through a deeper understanding of each style, we will become more effective at incorporating the different styles into our own sermons, and thus become more faithful proclaimers of the gospel.

Interestingly enough, there have been corresponding images associated with each of these preaching styles. The biblical teacher who most often envisions him- or herself as an expositor has often been referred to as a herald. The topical preacher who likes to consider the needs of the listener has been most readily represented by the image of pastor. And the teacher who gravitates toward narrative preaching has been most frequently depicted by the image of a storyteller. These images will prove to be helpful as we probe more deeply into these three styles of preaching.

the preacher as herald

Thomas Long poignantly addresses the preacher as herald in his book *The Witness of Preaching*: "A herald has but two responsibilities: to get the message straight and to speak it plainly. The king tells the herald what to proclaim, and the herald is obedient only to the extent that the king's word is delivered faithfully and without alteration."[1]

The image of the herald is a biblical one derived from several Greek terms in the New Testament that describe preaching, such as *kerusso* (κηρυσσω). The biblical image for the herald gained most of its prominence as a result of the neoorthodox theological movement of those who followed Karl Barth. Barth considered himself a herald and defined proclamation of the gospel as human language in and through which God himself speaks, like a king through the mouth of his herald, which moreover is meant to be heard and apprehended in faith as the divine acquittal, the eternal law and the eternal gospel both together.[2]

In Barth's view, the Bible is inspired, and though it may contain some errors because of the human involvement in its inception, it has the ability to become the Word of God in existential encounters. Consequently, heralds have one primary purpose: delivering the invading Word of God in specific encounters to the people who have ears to hear. This is why the herald is typically associated with the expository preacher.

However, it must be said that not all proponents of an expository style follow strictly in the tradition of Barth. Rather, other heralds have frequently been proponents of what academics and theologians have termed "verbal, plenary inspiration," or the idea that the divine inspiration of the Bible extends not only to the thoughts expressed in the Bible (verbal), but also to each and every word used in the Bible to express those thoughts (plenary). This view assumes a higher level of inerrancy ("error-free-ness") than the Barthian and neoorthodox view, but the application remains the same: the herald is charged with delivering God's Word as God first delivered it.

In the excellent work titled *Concise Encyclopedia of Preaching*, William H. Willimon and Richard Lischer offer one of the most comprehensive reference works ever written on Christian preaching. Willimon and Lischer comment extensively on the historic style of expository preaching: "'Exposition' means bringing out what is there. The word exposition derives from the Latin word *expositio*, which means 'setting forth' or 'making accessible.' The expository sermon is a sermon which faithfully brings a message out of scripture and makes the message accessible to contemporary hearers."[3]

Though a concise definition like the one above is helpful as a launching pad from which to understand expository preaching, further clarification regarding its nature as a style must be made, given that it has been around so long. The problem, however, is attempting to precisely describe one, uniform style of expository sermon. It is like trying to "describe the United States Congress and how it works."[4] In reality, most people believe in good expository preaching, but few can adequately describe its workings. Of all the attempts to do so, Haddon Robinson has made one of the best efforts. He states, "Expository preaching is the communication of a biblical concept, derived from and transmitted through a historical, grammatical, and literary study of a passage in its context, which the Holy Spirit first applies to the personality and experience of the preacher, then through the preacher, applies to the hearers."[5]

The beauty of Robinson's definition is its focus upon the Word first, then the preacher. In 2 Timothy 4:2, the apostle Paul instructed young Timothy to "preach the Word." *Preach* means to herald, exhort, or cry out the very Word of the living God, hence the image of the herald that has become synonymous with the expository preacher. The herald's authority, like all faithful preaching, is derived from the Word. However, though Robinson's statement is certainly poignant and properly motivated, it cannot be said that every expository sermon is necessarily biblical because of its style. In fact, by expository preaching, I do not mean biblical preaching. Despite the fact that some fundamental and expository preachers claim that any style other than their own is unbiblical, this is simply not the case. All styles of preaching, including the heralded expository style, when in the hands of an unfaithful preacher, run the risk of being unbiblical.

Furthermore, given that Scripture is fundamentally a redemptive story centering on God's glory through his Son Jesus Christ and played out in the familial context of the church for the blessing of the world, we can emphatically state that any sermon is unbiblical if it preaches something short of that purpose. This means that while there is a place for moral, political, social, and even economic commentary within a sermon, such commentary ought never to be the central point of the sermon, no matter if that sermon's style is expository or otherwise. The redemptive work of Jesus Christ must always be the central point of our sermons, regardless of the style we use.

the historical divide
in expository preaching

The history of expository preaching has been divided into two periods. The division is due to the obvious differences between historical exposition and more modern styles of expository preaching. Such a distinction has therefore created a bit of confusion as to what constitutes expository preaching today. As mentioned in the introduction, Fred Craddock's *As One without Authority* marked a turning point in the world of homiletics. With regard to expository preaching, it divided such preaching into historical (pre-1971) and contemporary periods (post-1971). The distinction helps clarify the differences within the expository camp of preachers. For example, we can see how different the preaching of men like Charles Spurgeon and G. Campbell Morgan was from the preaching of Chuck Swindoll. While these three preachers would be considered expository heralds of the gospel, their styles are radically different. In an effort to find the common ground among all those who lean toward an expository style, I will define expository preaching as preaching in such a way that the teacher continuously and consistently draws the attention of the listener back to a given and governing passage of Scripture. This definition holds true in both historical periods.

biblical and theological precedents in expository preaching

Christian expository preaching finds its origins in the Bible itself. The use of oral lecture in the synagogue services of worship readily focused the listener's attention on passages from the Hebrew Torah. This expository trait united Judaism and the church in the early days of the Christian movement.

The reading and exposition of Scripture were parts of the synagogue service, together with liturgical sentences, prayers, and benedictions. For example, the Shema, Shemoneh Esreh, Kedushah, psalms, and hymns were all a part of Israel's worship of God. The Law and the Prophets were both read on the Sabbath day; however, when Hebrew ceased to be the spoken language, an interpretation became necessary as a supplement to the reading.[6] The sermon, therefore, began as an interpretive and instructive exposition of the Hebrew Scriptures. When Ezra read the Law in Nehemiah 8, he was assisted by the Levites who taught the people. For a long time no distinction was made between preaching and teaching; *teaching* was a common term in the synagogue, used also to describe Jesus' proclamation (Mark 1:21; Matt. 5:1–2). Rich expository literature arose out of this teaching in the synagogue, which is now known as the Targum, the Midrash, and the Haggadah. The substance of the tradition grew, and scriptural exposition was changed into a study of Scripture, which, unfortunately, often forgot the spirit of the letter.[7]

As we approach the New Testament, however, we see that Jesus' sermon in the synagogue at Nazareth became the most important link in a chain uniting Jewish proclamation and the Christian sermon, thereby bringing deep, expository continuity to the history of the biblical revelation. When Jesus preached his first inaugural sermon in the synagogue (Luke 4:18–21), he stood up and preached only after he drew the congregation's attention to Isaiah 61:1–2. Amazingly, Jesus' first sermon was not even his own words but rather words already spoken and recorded in the Hebrew Bible. In fact, Luke recorded Jesus' own words, his "sermon," consisting of only nine words: "Today this Scripture has been fulfilled in your hearing" (Luke 4:21 ESV).

In his preaching ministry, Jesus routinely employed the use of Hebrew Scripture in order to expositionally and faithfully preach an already existent Word. This reminds all of us who are called to preach that we do not need to come up with something new in the preaching process. Solid, biblical preaching is not based on clever creations of the new but rather faithful proclamations of the old gospel story of Jesus. As John Stott said so long ago in *Between Two Worlds*, "It is God's speech which makes our speech necessary."[8]

Though Jesus' expository preaching from the Hebrew Bible was accomplished with his own individual style of narrative and topical parable, it is undeniable that the message Jesus taught was in continuity with the flow of Hebrew thought and Scripture. After all, Jesus was a Jew, a child of Israel. Through that Jewish heritage, he inherited the Law and the Prophets. As a result, Jesus preached expository messages about the kingdom of God, messages that found their authority grounded in the

Hebrew Scriptures. Incidentally, Jesus' exposition of Old Testament Scripture was not "old style" verse by verse but rather an intriguing combination of topical and narrative exposition with an inductive flair as opposed to the more popular deductive sermon progression.

The apostle Paul, after his encounter with and subsequent conversion by Jesus, became one of the greatest preachers in the New Testament, employing Hebrew Scripture expositionally as a way of preaching the message of Jesus Christ. More so than any other New Testament writer, Paul was always looking to the past Word of God in order to preach the present and future message of Jesus Christ. For example, he took the theme of his famous letter to the Romans, "the righteous will live by faith," directly from Habakkuk 2:4. In Galatians 3, Paul reached way back into the annals of Hebrew Scripture and used the covenantal relationship between Yahweh and Abraham to preach about the church's righteousness by faith in Jesus Christ. This was a routine but still amazing hermeneutical move on his part. In fact, in the next chapter he continued this expository hermeneutic as he used the Old Testament story of Hagar and Sarah as an allegory to enable the church to understand that her people are now "children of promise" as a result of Christ's crucifixion and resurrection (Gal. 4:28).

The other apostles also exposited Scripture. Great expository sermons and introductions by Peter and Philip are found in

Acts 2:14–36 and Acts 8:26–35 respectively. The fact is that Jesus, Paul, Peter, and all of the New Testament writers communicated expositionally, for they each used the Hebrew Bible as the backdrop for their teachings. They did not see themselves as lone rangers, content to muse about their own thoughts and opinions, but rather would not consider preaching about God and his kingdom without standing firmly on his Word.[9]

Jesus as the ultimate herald

In John 14, Jesus displayed the image of herald and, in the process, provided further justification for an exegetical style of preaching. In accordance with John's expressed intent of having his readers "believe that Jesus is the Christ, the Son of God, and that by believing you may have life in his name" (John 20:31), he recorded Jesus eloquently heralding the coming kingdom of God. For example, at the end of chapter 13, Jesus had foretold Peter's denial of him, which no doubt brought sorrow to Peter's heart and uncertainty to the other disciples. After all, if Peter, the fiery leader of the disciples who might best be described as a "ready, fire, aim" kind of guy, was going to deny Jesus so blatantly, then the other disciples didn't stand a chance of remaining faithful. And so Jesus responded with words of reassurance that boldly heralded the kingdom of God:

"Let not your hearts be troubled. Believe in God; believe also in me. In my Father's house are many rooms. If it were not so, would I have told you that I go to prepare a place for you? And if I go and prepare a place for you, I will come again and will take you to myself, that where I am you may be also. And you know the way to where I am going." Thomas said to him, "Lord, we do not know where you are going. How can we know the way?" Jesus said to him, "I am the way, and the truth, and the life. No one comes to the Father except through me." (John 14:1–6 ESV)

The four Gospels are laced with Jesus heralding the message of God. In the case of John 14, he was heralding a clear message about the kingdom of God and how to enter it. Modern-day heralds of the gospel, likewise, live to proclaim and prioritize the explanation of the person, work, and words of Jesus, just as they are delivered in Scripture.

extrabiblical precedents in expository preaching

One of the reasons why expository preaching often receives harsh criticism is because critics see it as an old, outdated style of preaching. Indeed, as I have noted above, expository preaching is by far the earliest and most widely used method in the history of modern preaching.

The Greek expository homily never rose to greater heights than it did during the fourth century under John Chrysostom, the patriarch of Constantinople. Chrysostom became known to the world by the name Golden Mouth. Together with men like Savonarola and Luther, Chrysostom became one of the giant figures in the history of preaching. In fact, Pope Pius X designated him the patron saint of preachers because of his expository form.

Chrysostom was not the only great expositor in pre-Reformation extra-canonical history. The list also includes Cyprian, Athanasius, Augustine, the Venerable Bede, Bernard of Clairvaux, and John Wyclif. During the Reformation, however, expository preaching underwent a revival as heralds such as Ulrich Zwingli, Martin Bullinger, and John Calvin preached through entire books of the Bible, verse by verse. They, along with post-Reformation scholars like John Wesley, Karl Barth, and Helmut Thielicke, all vigorously employed an expository style of preaching so as to "increase the level of biblical literacy in the life of the church."[10]

The "golden chain" of expository heralds continues to link the gospel of Jesus Christ to his bride, the church. Many other expository preachers of the past, like Charles Spurgeon and G. Campbell Morgan, have greatly advanced the kingdom of God.

And through modern-day preachers such as Chuck Swindoll and Haddon Robbinson, faithful expository preaching is still alive and well in the church today.

strengths of expository preaching

The hallmark of expository preaching is that it almost always focuses on "speaking the one word humanity most urgently and desperately needs to hear."[11] Expository preaching strives to focus hearers on the Word of the Lord by remaining fixed on one governing passage of Scripture throughout the message.

An obvious strength of the expository method is the high theological view of preaching that this style communicates. In Romans 10:14–15, Paul rhetorically asked about the theology of preaching: "How, then, can they call on the one they have not believed in? And how can they believe in the one of whom they have not heard? And how can they hear without someone preaching to them? And how can they preach unless they are sent? As it is written, 'How beautiful are the feet of those who bring good news!'"

Heralds of the expository style are committed to a high theological view of preaching. Everything about the style communicates the importance of the Word and, therefore, the importance and authority of the one whom God has called to deliver the Word. While other styles of biblical proclamation also strive to reach these ends, expository preachers tend to communicate this theology at a higher pitch when they discuss the role of the Bible in sermon delivery.

theological diagram
of expository preaching

This high theological view of preaching and extreme commitment to the biblical text found in expository sermons is captured in the figure below. This style of preaching understands the "invading" quality of God's Word coming down from heaven and being transmitted through the authors of Scripture, who themselves were charged with divinely recording that Word in such a way as to point their audience to the person and work of Christ. Similarly, the Word continues to be delivered through present-day preachers who are also charged with pointing their audiences to the person and work of Christ in hopes of bringing about an intellectual and spiritual wrestling with the gospel that leads to repentance, faith, and ultimately salvation.

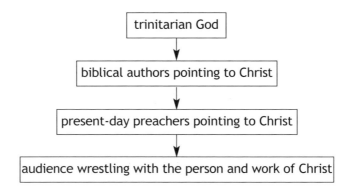

As the diagram demonstrates, heralds believe the best way to ensure direct deliverance of God's plan is direct, authoritative delivery of the Word. James Packer describes this expository pursuit in preaching when he says, "Preaching appears in the Bible as a relaying of what God has said about himself and his doings, and about men in relation to him, plus a pressing of his commands, promises, warnings, and assurances, with a view to winning the hearer or hearers . . . to a positive response."[12] The emphasis is on relaying the Word.

Historical, expository heralds typically talk little about interpretation, human needs, and hermeneutical leaps from biblical text to sermon. According to the herald, in true exposition the emphasis is much more about rightly delivering the biblical text that is already on the pages of Holy Writ. As John MacArthur boldly suggests, this is after all "the only logical response to inerrant Scripture."[13]

Some view this kind of theological reasoning and biblical interpretation as a weakness. While I am not willing to echo MacArthur's assertion that this is the only response to Scripture, I do believe the heightened theological underpinnings related to expository preaching in the church is a strength preachers cannot afford to lose. In a day of religious pluralism, and biblical skepticism and illiteracy, any style that heightens the theological significance of the Word and those who seek to deliver that Word can and should be considered a strength.

Another pertinent strength, particularly in this day and age, is the biblically didactic nature of expository preaching. In a day when mainline churches are in decline, baby boomers and busters are returning to the church, often having not attended in more than a decade. Preachers in the twenty-first century are trying to proclaim the Bible in a culture where mass religious pluralism invades every aspect of Western society. Into this context, the didactic or teaching quality of expository preaching is an invaluable asset in the church. As far back as Moses, Israel, and the Shema, God's people have understood the significance of teaching the words of Holy Scripture:

Hear, O Israel: The LORD our God, the LORD is one. You shall love the LORD your God with all your heart and with all your soul and with all your might. And these words that

I command you today shall be on your heart. You shall teach them diligently to your children, and shall talk of them when you sit in your house, and when you walk by the way, and when you lie down, and when you rise. You shall bind them as a sign on your hand, and they shall be as frontlets between your eyes. You shall write them on the doorposts of your house and on your gates. (Deut. 6:4–9 ESV)

Clearly, Moses and ancient Israel understood the centrality of God's Word so much that they wanted to physically place that Word throughout their homes and in the life of the community. Expository preaching has always emphasized and continues to emphasize the centrality of the Bible and the preacher's responsibility to teach the Word of God.

While receiving my doctorate at Asbury Theological Seminary, I studied over twenty classical sermons in each of the three predominant styles. To learn from each style, identifying their nuances, strengths, and weaknesses, I immersed myself in the best sermons of each category.

With regards to the exposition, I studied twenty sermons by Charles Spurgeon, G. Campbell Morgan, and Chuck Swindoll. All three of these heralds of the gospel exhibited a commitment to faithfully teaching the Scriptures during sermon delivery. Of the three, I personally found Swindoll to be most captivating. For example, he demonstrates a unique teaching quality in his collection of sermons entitled *Laugh Again*.[14] The first sermon I read by Dr. Swindoll was "The Hidden Secret of a Happy Life."[15] As a contemporary herald of exposition, Swindoll seems to set himself apart from some of the more historical heralds like Spurgeon and Morgan. Dr. Swindoll consults a host of sources and incorporates these outside sources into the DNA building blocks of his sermons. For example, in this one sermon, Dr. Swindoll incorporates insight from the following sources or fields of study: ancient Rome, religion, Epicureanism, education, psychology, materialism, ascetism, humanism, pride, Harry A. Ironside, Martin Lloyd-Jones, and Tom Landry. Dr. Swindoll hermeneutically maneuvers between the biblical text, the hearer, and the world in which the listener lives with seamless communication and skill.

In another sermon, "Freeing Yourself Up to Laugh Again,"[16] Swindoll continues to mount didactic evidence for his case, while all the time penetrating the biblical text at hand and the predicament in which the listener lives. Once he discusses Philippians 4:4–7, he then exhausts seven full pages mining for nuggets of truth found deep within the field of God's Word. In doing so, he brings new meaning to the educational and penetrating focus of expository preaching. As the sermon comes to a close, Dr. Swindoll's three final points are: feed your mind positive thoughts, focus your attention on encouraging models, and find the "God of Peace" in every situation.

Dr. Swindoll, along with the other heralds mentioned above, demonstrates an unyielding commitment to a didactic and faithful adherence to the Word of God. While historical and contemporary heralds differ in their consideration for the listener and his or her needs, each masterfully preaches the Word of God with a keen sense of seriousness and intentional focus on the biblical text.

weaknesses of expository preaching

Lots of ink has been spilled in the last thirty years on the various weaknesses of expository preaching. The new era of homiletics, to which I referred earlier, was ushered into existence by Fred Craddock. However, Craddock does not deserve all the blame or applause for this major shift in the homiletical landscape since many preachers, professors, and laity have desired freshness in the pulpit. A call for a new form was specifically ushered into existence between 1960 and 1970. This period was a time of homiletical experimentation and reaction. The sermon, however, was not the sole target for revolution, as many churches also experimented with music, art, and architecture. Now that the dust has settled, many are beginning to understand that the expository method was not totally inadequate, though it does bear weaknesses.

ignoring the hearer's context

The first major weakness evident in the history of expository preaching is its failure to adequately consider the context of the hearer and the church during a particular time and place. To preach in the era of Christendom, say in the early- to mid-twentieth century, was far different than preaching in the twenty-first century. During the Christendom era, the majority of Americans claimed to be Christians. In fact, some have tried to make the case that being an American was synonymous with being a Christian. Granted, Christendom was a time in which people came to church enthusiastically interested in the things of God. Christians flocked to church and sat on hard, wooden pews listening to sermons that lasted one, two, and sometimes three or more hours. Christian parishioners were interested in biblical content and were willing to sit under the authoritative preacher boldly proclaiming the whole counsel of God's Word. Those days are long gone.

Unfortunately, the Western world has become individualistic and obsessed with itself. The focus is no longer "we," the church, and the knowledge and application of God's Word. Rather, the focus is now "I," my family, and what the Bible says to meet my needs and how it can help me become a better person. In short, the fundamental shift is from God and his Word to me and my needs. Needless to say, this kind of individualism and consumerism has been shattering to preconceived notions of sermon attendance and attention. Let me be clear, both individualism and consumerism are diametrically opposed to authentic Christian community as described in the Bible. However, that does not negate the fact that it is in the water we drink and, quite possibly, more popular today than it has ever been before. The fundamental question, therefore, becomes: Do preachers, as a result of the radical individualism invading American culture, alter, adjust, adopt, or totally abandon their style of preaching?

Jesus, the greatest preacher ever, carefully considered context and the needs of those who gathered around him. One read through the Gospels and you'll notice that Jesus never preached or taught the same way twice. While his method of parabolic storytelling was consistent, Jesus always took seriously the contextual needs of those who came to hear the good news. Unfortunately, expository preaching has traditionally neglected this practice. Expository preachers have been so consumed with exegeting the Word that they have failed to exegete the culture and the people in the pews. While this tendency seems to elevate the Bible to a place of prominence in the community, it just might leave the Word there, elevated to loftiness without application in the lives of those gathered to hear. Furthermore, what seems to be an elevated view of the Word might actually be a diminished view, since God's Word was never meant to be some esoteric collection of literature void of application. Thus, teaching without the audience in mind undermines the very purpose of God's Word.

For example, in the sermon "Sanctification,"[17] the great herald of the gospel, G. Campbell Morgan, exhausted nine single-spaced pages discussing sanctification. The sermon is pregnant with truth regarding the sanctifying work of God. The weakness, however, resides in the fact that this sermon could have been preached anywhere during the nineteenth century, and the reader would not have known the difference. That is, while the sermon was full of Christian truth, the preacher never once contextualized the message for a particular people at a particular place during a particular time. As such, this same kind of sermon today would lack the contextual specificity needed to engage postmodern people who think only in terms of their own context. While few expository preachers still deliver these kinds of noncontextualized sermons, the reality remains that this thread of neglect still runs deep into the fabric of expository preaching and therefore is viewed as a weakness.

deemphasizes rhetoric

The second major weakness of the expository style of preaching is its lack of concern for rhetoric. Ironically, heralds tend to understand this neglect as intentional and admirable. Their focus is proclaiming the pure Word and delivering that which is printed on the page. Therefore, strict expository preachers see little need for rhetorical or stylistic concern. Granted, this theology sounds admirable. The only problem is that it fails to realize, as was mentioned in the historical survey of preaching, that Scripture itself was first contextualized and written with great concern for rhetoric.

The Word of God was and will always be an event, a happening in history with creative power.[18] Such power, therefore, is certainly not devoid of rhetoric and style, no matter how admirable it might seem to assume otherwise. As W. M. Urban states, when "we abandon linguistic forms in order to grasp reality, that reality, like quicksilver, runs through our fingers."[19] As preachers and teachers, we ought to feel permitted and even empowered to employ linguistic rhetoric for the purpose of communicating the truths of God's Word.

The oral nature of the original Scriptures forced later biblical writers to be concerned not only with faithfully recording those Scriptures, but recording them in a way that preserved the rhetorical elements through which they were originally transmitted. Expository preachers who critique any concern for rhetoric and linguistic style must reckon with the fact that in the Bible an intentional concern for the very things they disparage are not only found throughout, but are a part of what makes the Scriptures so powerful and fascinating. As one New Testament scholar states, "The rhetorical dimensions of the gospel were not mere ornaments designed to make the message more attractive, but rather they were forms called forth by the nature of the gospel itself."[20]

authoritarian clericalism

The last, but surely not least, weakness of expository preaching that we will discuss for the purposes of this book derives from the way in which expository deduction provides homiletical support for authoritarian and arrogant clericalism. Within an expository sermon, thought and logic move in two directions between experience and truth. Inductive reasoning moves from experience to the general truth; deductive reasoning moves from the general truth to the application or experience of that truth.

inductive: experience $\longrightarrow$ general truth

deductive: general truth $\longrightarrow$ application (experience)

Deductive reasoning usually dominates in expository preaching. However, the deductive style of preaching presupposes an authoritarian herald of the gospel and a passive listener in the pew, both of which are dying parts of the past. While many preachers still yearn in the quiet corners of their hearts for this kind of authority, the reality is that few people grant the church or its leaders that kind of authority anymore. Plus, the days of passive listening are long gone. Postmodern people have an insatiable desire to engage, experience, evaluate, and decide truth for themselves. Whether this kind of radical individualism is good or bad is always up for debate. As I have already stated, it is incompatible with the interdependence of authentic Christian community. Nevertheless, it is reality, and effective preachers must decide whether or not they are going to meet postmodern Christians or seekers where they are and move them to faithfulness or leave them there to die in their individualism and ultimately their sin. Following the example of Christ, I believe, requires that preachers meet them where they are, which in all likelihood requires that we adjust our understanding of expository preaching in order to engage the hearer in dialogue and conversation. The fact that strict expository deduction fails to do this is a weakness of epic proportions.

testing the strengths and weaknesses of expository preaching

For my doctoral dissertation in seminary, I wrestled with this question of what constitutes expository preaching in comparison to topical or narrative preaching. The wrestling provoked me to engage in a personalized, statistical analysis, which sought to determine the most effective style of preaching with all other things being equal.

I established a group of thirty-two laypeople from new**hope** church who became the sermon research team for this project. We met once a month for a period of a year to talk about preaching styles and for them to provide me with quality feedback and data. Primarily, the sermon research team agreed to be present for twelve sermons, four of each of the three styles. The sermon research team was incredibly gracious and helpful in statistically evaluating these twelve sermons based on engagement with the sermon, ability to memorize Scripture, and the effectiveness of sustained and real-life application. The three constant ingredients in this research project were the new church plant known as new**hope**, my role as the communicator, and the use of multimedia.

I began the project by preaching four expository sermons on Sundays at new**hope** church. The first expository sermon in the research was a sermon on Philippians 1:27—2:16 titled "Finding Joy in All the Wrong Places!" In true expository form, the point of the sermon was to lead the congregation through the Philippians passage, teaching that true joy is acquired when we take on the attitude of Christ and serve others. To do so, I set the biblical passage in its original context first, then addressed the lack of joy that most people experience in this day and age, intentionally inserted humor, and then expositionally exhorted the congregation based primarily on Philippians 2:1–16.

For the purpose of enhancing the exposition, I used a flip chart to demonstrate the way in which we serve in the footsteps of Christ and in the end will be exalted as he was (Phil. 2:9–11). I then turned the sermon toward application and employed an acrostic for JOY in order to teach the congregation about priorities in life: Jesus, Others, and Yourself. Finally, the congregation was invited to receive Communion, and by faith, prioritize their lives in this order. The sermon stayed true to the text and didn't wander among other scriptural passages but rather expositionally exhorted the congregation to join Paul in participating in this Christ hymn. On a scale of one to four, with one being most expository and four being least expository, the sermon research team ranked this sermon first among the four sermons.

The second expository sermon was a sermon on John 8:1–11. The broader context for this particular sermon was a sermon series entitled CSI (Christ Scenes Investigated). As the title implies, this series took poignant scenes from the life and ministry of Jesus Christ and developed worship services around those biblical passages. This particular sermon focused on the passage where the Pharisees confronted Jesus with a woman caught in adultery. The sermon began and ended with references to skipping stones. With that reference in mind, I began by sharing a personal story from my life in which I could have been accused of throwing stones with the Pharisees. The story afforded me the opportunity to begin by connecting with many who have struggled with being judgmental and conclude, inductively with the statement, "I've never been good at skipping stones." To help visualize the sermon, I used large stones on the stage as props and used stone imagery in the graphics for my teaching.

While the beginning and the end of the sermon were creatively tied together and fit the theme in the biblical text (throwing stones), the sermon was not the most expository sermon. To discuss an issue like sexuality in a postmodern church, I had to spend time discussing sexuality according to Scripture as opposed to sexuality according to our culture. And while the sermon did not wander throughout Scripture, it also did not continually take the congregation back to the text in a verse-by-verse fashion, which is typically the way expository sermons are defined. Rather, the sermon text itself served as a springboard from which I addressed sexuality, faithfulness, and grace as opposed to judgmentalism. As such, this particular expository sermon ranked third in relation to the other expository sermons.

The third expository sermon came within a series titled "Soul Survivor." The sermon was enhanced with a stage completely decorated as a jungle, including tiki torches, trees, and the like. The biblical text for the sermon was Matthew 6:19–24 and its theme of stewardship. The main thrust of the message came from the verse, "Do not lay up for yourselves treasures on earth, where moth and rust destroy and where thieves break in and steal, but lay up for yourselves treasures in heaven, where neither moth nor rust destroys and where thieves do not break in and steal. For where your treasure is, there your heart will be also" (Matt. 6:19–21 ESV).

In discussing an issue like money with a new church, I felt compelled to integrate into the message other passages of Scripture. As such, this particular sermon ended up being not so much an expository sermon on Matthew 6:19–24 as a topical message on money, with the use of Matthew 6:19–24 as a primary passage. Stylistically, the sermon research team concluded that this could not be counted as an expository sermon and therefore should not be considered in this research. On the same rating scale, this particular sermon clearly ranked fourth among the four sermons.

The fourth expository sermon came on the Sunday before Christmas. We were in the middle of a message series titled, "Return of the King—The Journey Continues." The biblical passage in focus was John 1:1–5, 14. True to the expository style, I stayed grounded to the Johannine text. Since it was the Sunday before Christmas, I talked about watershed events taking place at the time—events like the capture of Saddam Hussein and the hundredth-year anniversary of the Wright brothers' flight and the celebration that took place at Kitty Hawk, North Carolina, the week prior. I intentionally juxtaposed these events with the greatest of all watershed events, the birth of Jesus Christ. I expositionally led the congregation through John 1:1–5, 14, making the following points:

1. Jesus journeyed from heaven to earth (John 1:3).
2. Jesus journeyed from eternity to time (John 1:1).
3. Jesus journeyed from heaven to spirit and body (John 1:14).
4. Jesus journeyed from deity to humanity (John 1:1).

Overall, the sermon took a very straightforward approach, using John 1 to theologically demonstrate the world-changing significance of the incarnation. This sermon came in second among the four expository sermons.

expository preaching test findings

When these sermons were evaluated based on the rankings mentioned above, the data from the sermon research team found that expository sermons scored lower than the other two styles of sermons on all items relating to engagement. As predicted and as mentioned in the weaknesses of expository sermons, these sermons were somewhat less engaging than the other two styles.

What is more fascinating, however, is the fact that these expository sermons had a greater impact on the listeners' ability to memorize Scripture than either the topical or narrative sermons, even though they were deemed less engaging. That is, when the participants were asked specific questions about their ability to memorize biblical passages from the expository sermons delivered, they were much more apt to do so than with the topical or narrative sermons. Overall, the results suggest that expository preaching may help believers become better students of the Word, but it is found wanting in applying those truths to everyday living. It tends to help listeners learn and remember Scripture, but lacks engagement and the ability to apply the Scripture they have learned to their daily lives.

As you might imagine, it is extremely helpful to know the strengths and weaknesses of a particular style of sermon. As such, the preacher is able to think through his or her goals of a particular message and then move toward the style that most facilitates a desired response or application. Now let's turn to the ever-growing and popular style of topical preaching.

pastor:
topical preaching

5

As a result of my time in the Beeson Pastor Program at Asbury Theological Seminary, I have been introduced to and interacted with pastors serving in some of the largest and most effective churches in the world. During conversations with these great leaders and while sitting under their teaching, I noticed a trend with only few exceptions. The trend is that almost all of these pastors preach topical sermons; an interesting phenomenon, no doubt. If the purpose of the church is to reach people for Jesus, and one of the primary ways in which God has always accomplished that mission is through faithful preaching, then we would do well to "go to school" on this ever-increasing, popular style of Christian preaching.

the preacher as pastor

Topical preaching has long been represented by the image of the preacher as pastor. There is more to this than naming a person in a clerical position. The preaching style actually takes on a pastoral presence as the teacher addresses the needs of the people. Engrained in this image is the notion that he or she "deliberately sets out to touch, involve, and address people's personal concerns."[1] This is why the pastor is typically associated with topical preaching. A pastor will often use relevant biblical topics as a launching pad from which to connect to the personal concerns of the people. When one is preaching pastorally, one is attuned to the needs of the hearers, the fallen condition we possess as the result of our sin nature. For the preaching pastor, these needs—but not necessarily wants of the congregation—take on much more prominence than they do for the herald. Through a given biblical topic, the pastor discerns these needs, even diagnoses these needs, and then strives to be of help by intervening with the gospel and speaking a scriptural word that clarifies the repentance and faith in Jesus Christ that ultimately can bring restoration. Topical preachers pride themselves on being relevant and in touch with the times. Karl Barth was once asked what he did to prepare his Sunday sermon. Barth answered, "I take the Bible in one hand and the daily newspaper in the other."[2] This is the kind of cultural relevance that is encouraged in topical preaching.

Two other implications of the pastor image for the nature and practice of preaching should be considered. First, while for the herald the most important dimension of preaching is the message that has the power to bring repentance and faith, for the pastor the crucial dimension for preaching is an event centered on repentance and faith happening inside the hearer. The pastor of topical preaching hopes to teach in such a way that he or she connects the transformative gospel of Jesus Christ to the fallen condition and sin-based needs of the hearer.

Second, if the herald image deemphasizes the person and presence of the preacher, the pastor image reemphasizes it. The pastor image implies that the preacher's relationship to the hearers, in terms of style, personality, character, and previous experiences, is a crucial dimension of the pastoral and therapeutic process. In his book *The Minister as Shepherd*, Charles Jefferson states the perspective of the pastor-preacher succinctly when he says, "The city must be saved and they are to be saved by shepherds."[3] Summarizing Jefferson's book, Warren Wiersbe said: "Let the preacher be a pastor and the flock will strengthen itself and increase."[4] The faithful topical preacher, therefore, quite often uses a pastoral style in delivering the Word of the Lord.

the nature of topical preaching

When I use the phrase "topical sermon" what I mean is that the teacher is free to choose a text from the Bible rather than preach on a passage assigned by a lectionary.[5] Topical preachers will often begin with a theme or topic in mind and then turn to a biblical text to help define and explain the topic. In other words, rather than starting with the text to develop the message, preachers begin first with a message that needs to be heard through a biblical text or texts.

Consequently, in order for a topical sermon to be faithful, the pastor must make sure the topic is itself biblical and therefore connected to faithful exegesis of a particular passage of the Bible that addresses the topic. When done well, topical preaching is able to view personal issues of the church through a biblical perspective and worldview, thus bringing a strong pastoral side to the sermon. When done poorly, pastors choose their agendas and then go scanning the biblical terrain compiling enough references to warrant speaking on a topic in a manner that only appears to be a sermon. In order to avoid this, topical preachers, like all preachers, need to have an adequate understanding of the whole counsel of God as contained in the Old and New Testaments.

Jesus as the ultimate pastor

In Matthew 18, the disciples came to Jesus with a question with which we can totally resonate. They asked Jesus, "Who is the greatest in the kingdom of heaven?" (Matt. 18:1). In other words, "Jesus, in the Super Bowl of life, are you taking the Patriots or the Steelers? Are you a Microsoft or Apple kind of guy? What's the over-under on UNC vs. Duke?" And with the perfect pastoral tone Jesus responded, "Truly, I say to you, unless you turn and become like children, you will never enter the kingdom of heaven. Whoever humbles himself like this child is the greatest in the kingdom of heaven" (Matt. 18:3–4 ESV). Then, as if an analogy about little children was not pastoral enough, Jesus added an analogy about helpless, little sheep under the care of a loving shepherd. He said, "What do you think? If a man has a hundred sheep, and one of them has gone astray, does he not leave the ninety-nine on the mountains and go in search of the one that went astray? And if he finds it, truly, I say to you, he rejoices over it more than over the ninety-nine that never went astray. So it is not the will of my Father who is in heaven that one of these little ones should perish" (Matt. 18:12–14 ESV).

Notice how Jesus embodied a pastoral presence as he addressed the topics of the day. He perceived the need of his disciples: encouragement, through a proper understanding of grace (rather than achievement) as the means for entrance into the kingdom. He then entered into that need without catering to it. For example, though Jesus affirmed the disciples' question, he showed them how their understanding of the question was flawed and that it is not greatness but grace and childlike humility that secures one's place in heaven. Finally, he enhanced his connection with his hearers by using the analogy of a shepherd seeking out a single lost sheep to further model his pastoral presence in the lives of the disciples. As we note how Jesus preached and taught in topical and pastoral fashion, the implication for us seems to be clear: Do not neglect the needs and concerns of the hearer lest you forsake the ability and opportunity to speak the gospel into a listener's heart and mind.

biblical precedents in topical preaching

Many people today incorrectly assume that topical preaching is a recent invention that enjoys popularity most extensively and exclusively in megachurch circles. While topical preaching is most prominent today among megachurches and their pastors, this style of preaching, like the other two, has its roots in the soil of the biblical narrative. As already mentioned in chapter 4, Jesus often preached expository sermons to draw his audience's attention back to particular texts within the Hebrew Bible. Scholars have also noted how Jesus frequently preached narrative messages by using parables and inadvertent induction plots. What is most often neglected is the way in which Jesus allowed the needs of the hearers to determine his topic for preaching. When people would come to Jesus and ask questions or have certain needs, he refused to brush these people off as the Pharisees might have preferred. Instead he would rearrange his schedule or journey in order to address the needs of his people with the gospel message. In other words, he would contextualize the gospel toward the needs of his hearers. It's an essentially topical approach that proved to be as faithful for proclaiming the Word of God as a verse-by-verse exposition, depending on the context.

Another strength of topical sermons, as Jesus' sermons show, is that they possess an incarnational element to them. In other words, they put "God's message in human garb," thereby giving it relevancy and personality.[6] This incarnational element is vividly seen in Matthew's gospel as Jesus' storytelling spins together a series of parables in Matthew 13. Here, Jesus taught parables pertaining to a sower (13:1–23), weeds in a field (13:24–30, 36–43), a mustard seed and yeast (13:31–35), hidden treasure and valuable pearl (13:44–46), and a fishing net (13:47–52). By preaching with parables, Jesus was able to teach in a manner that addressed the concerns and needs of his audiences, while allowing those same audiences to make the necessary connections between the meaning and applications of the parables themselves. His parabolic and essentially top-ical preaching enabled his hearers to take ownership of the message and more faithfully apply it to their lives. In this sense, Jesus was the ultimate topical preacher or pastor.

It must be noted however, that Jesus' method works coun-terintuitively and, in fact, goes against the grain of most of today's topical preaching. Contemporary topical preaching typically announces a topic in the beginning and then moves deductively through the sermon in such a way that pastors end up springboarding from one text to another in order to build a convincing case for that which they have already claimed in the introduction.

By contrast though, Jesus' first sermon in Matthew's gospel was inductive as opposed to deductive. And amazingly, these words were preached to none other than Satan himself. After Jesus was led into the wilderness to be tempted, Satan entered the scene and determined the topical agenda. In Matthew 4:3, 5, and 8, Satan introduced the topics of food, safety, and power, respectively. In response, Jesus did not retreat from the pro-posed topics. Rather, he embraced the topics, addressed them with the Hebrew Scriptures, and subsequently refocused them in light of God's value system in the kingdom.

Similarly, after officially beginning his ministry among the people, Jesus continued to use a topical approach to preaching and teaching, specifically with the Sermon on the Mount. While Jesus could have been content to hang out around the first church in Jerusalem and those disciples whom he had already called, he instead chose to go to those with particular needs. Specifically, he chose to live out most of his ministry up north around the Sea of Galilee, where he encountered poor beggars, those suffering with leprosy, the crippled, and those who had spiritual questions. Jesus' agenda becomes clear after one glance through the gospel narratives. It was to usher in the kingdom of God, which required tangible and spiritual pastoring of people and addressing their needs topically against the backdrop of the gospel as a foreshadowing of what was to come. What we find is that, like expository preaching, topical preaching also finds legitimate grounding in the words and ministry of Jesus.

extra-biblical precedents in topical preaching

Saint Augustine is credited with making the first formal defense of the use of rhetoric in preaching the gospel. James Cox notes, "Everything that Augustine said in favor of the art of rhetoric in preaching can be said in favor of topical preaching— and for similar reasons."[7] For Augustine, preaching was essentially a running commentary on Scripture texts. But as a teacher of rhetorical communication and art, Augustine was determined to preach the Word with creative innovation and concern for the listener, a hallmark of the topical preacher. His rationale was as follows: For since by means of the art of rhetoric both truth and falsehood are urged, who would dare to say that truth should stand in the person of its defenders unarmed against lying, so that they who wish to use falsehoods may know how to make their listeners benevolent, or attentive, or docile in their presentations, while the defenders of truth are ignorant of that art?[8]

Just as ancient rhetoric sought to compete for attention in the marketplace, topical preaching seeks to compete with the listeners' obsession with their needs and secular society's willingness to try to meet those needs. Good topical preaching chimes in with the plethora of marketplace voices, offering the unique and irreplaceable gospel balm for the wounds and hurts of real people. Good topical preaching is usually integrative; it reaches out in all possible directions for gospel substance that adequately addresses the issues or needs under consideration. Few preachers have practiced the topical style more effectively than contemporary preachers Clovis Chappell, Bill Hybels, Mike Breaux, Joyce Meyer, and John Ed Mathison. We will now turn to the strengths and weaknesses of topical preaching.

strengths of topical preaching

One strength already mentioned is that, like narrative and expository styles of sermon proclamation, topical preaching can also be traced directly back to Jesus Christ, whose sermons were often messages of kingdom truth given in response to various topics brought to him by the masses. Clearly, any style that finds Jesus as its model is valid and has the potential of winning souls and changing lives for the sake of God's kingdom.

A second strength of topical preaching is the immediate connection this style has with the unchurched and dechurched people among us. Even those we might consider never churched, who have no prior affiliation or experience with the Christian church, seem to appreciate when a pastor speaks to his or her unique topical needs.

People in the West are becoming increasingly secular and have been for some time. Along with this radical secularization comes a narcissistic individualism and crass consumerism. Those influenced in such a way unashamedly want to know if the church has anything to offer them. Topical messages have the potential of showing the unchurched, dechurched, and never churched among us that the answer is actually yes, that the church not only has something for them, but would be honored to speak with them about that something.

Bill Hybels powerfully demonstrates this point in one of his sermons from the series "What Makes a Man and What Makes a Woman." When Hybels and the elders of the church announced the sermon title in advance, they noticed a 20 percent increase in worship attendance the week of the actual sermon. Hybels states, "When that series ['What Makes a Man and What Makes a Woman'] ended, I began one titled, 'A Portrait of Jesus.' We lost most of the newcomers [who had begun attending during the former series]. Interestingly, the elders said to me after that series, 'Bill those messages on the person and the work of Christ related to the unchurched people as well as any messages we've heard.' In this case, the problem wasn't the content; the people who needed to hear this series most didn't come because of the title."[9]

Topical preaching, more so than expository and narrative preaching, attracts on average more secular people who may not otherwise darken the doors of a church building.

A third strength of topical preaching is that it enables the pastor to preach on innumerably rich texts in the Bible that are not covered by lectionary-based systems. Topical preaching actually opens up the larger biblical canon to preachers and, therefore, enables them to consider more faithfully the totality of God's Word.

Overall, topical preaching has an evangelistic lure and strength because it addresses people and their needs. As such it follows in the footsteps of Christ. The danger of topical preaching, however, is when it leaves the listener walking away with unresolved needs, or maybe worse, having his or her needs met by a pastor and his or her opinion as opposed to the Word of the Lord. To this and other weaknesses, we now turn.

weaknesses of topical preaching

Frequently, topical pastors choose need-meeting topics and then address those topics not by faithfully exegeting a particular text, but by using various passages of Scripture. If topical pastors are not careful, they can begin offering their perspective or worldview pertaining to the needs of the congregation based on proof texting from the Word of the Lord. Or, as I have seen on many occasions, the pastor wanders aimlessly outside the realm of Scripture and in doing so actually abandons its authority. That is why topical preaching can be a slippery slope, particularly if the pastor is not grounded in the Word of God. If not careful, one can start preaching messages that are not aligned with the whole scope of Scripture. There have been countless assaults on the Word in the history of the church and we should be extremely careful when engaging in topical preaching.

The simple but serious point is that topical preaching runs a greater risk than either expository or narrative preaching of becoming unbiblical and selling one's soul to the mass of individualistic "needs" so rampant in society today. Many years ago, Harry Emerson Fosdick warned of the topical preacher: "[They] search contemporary life in general and the newspapers in particular for subjects. . . . Instead of starting with a text, they start with their own ideas on some subject of their choice, but their ideas on that subject may be farther away from the vital interests of the people than a great text from the Bible."[10]

Interestingly enough, Fosdick was a topical preacher; however, Fosdick, like many topical preachers, knew the difference between faithfully preaching a topic addressed in the Word and pandering to the needs of people without consistent attention given to faithfully reading and teaching the Scriptures. Topical preaching, like expository and narrative, must find its authoritative origin within the biblical canon.

topical versus textual preaching

Identifying the difference between topical and textual preaching is appropriate at this point. The distinction between a textual and topical sermon largely has to do with the pastor's approach to the sermon. Richard Caemmerer demonstrates this when he says, "The textual sermon finds its theme and goal in a text. The topical sermon begins with a theme and goal in the mind of the preacher."[11] According to this distinction, the greatest potential weakness of topical preaching is making the Bible say what one wants it to say on a given topic, as opposed to faithfully preaching what the Bible wants you to say regarding that specific topic. There is a huge difference. To be quite candid, there are few topics more important than this when it comes to faithful preaching.

This weakness is not to imply that all topical preaching involves unfaithful proof texting, but simply that topical preaching has a greater proclivity for errors of this kind. When done well, though, both topical and textual preaching acknowledge the authority of Scripture, reflect biblical doctrine, and develop a biblical text. A pastor may discern a topic before deciding on a text, so long as he then appropriately locates and exegetes a governing passage of Scripture that adequately addresses the previously discerned topic. In this way, "The textual sermon brings the biblical to bear on the secular; the topical sermon puts the secular into the context of the biblical" as opposed to the other way around.[12]

Another weakness of topical preaching is that it promotes and reinforces, in a subtle way, individualism within the body of Christ. The important point to note here is how preaching to specific felt needs and topics of concern, whether preachers want to or not, can subtly communicate to the hearers that their needs are primary. If pastors are going to address the needs of God's people, they must be intentional in making sure those particular needs are adequately addressed within the Bible. In doing so, we help the laity learn to understand that Christianity's chief purpose is not to just meet our needs, but rather it often exposes the selfishness and sinfulness of our needs and replaces those needs with a sanctified life of learning how to resemble Jesus! If this message is not communicated, topical pastors are further legitimizing the individualistic consumerism of American culture. Granted, starting with the felt needs of the listener is an appropriate and faithful hermeneutical move in the preaching process; however, leaving the audience saturated in a never-ending list of needs communicates that the gospel is present only to serve us as opposed to the other way around. We can easily begin to see Jesus as our genie in a bottle instead of the Sovereign Lord of creation in whom we live, move, and have our being (Acts 17:28).

testing the strengths and weaknesses of topical preaching

As mentioned previously, I had the unbelievable privilege of planting new**hope** church in 2002. It was in this baby church that I identified eager hearers of the Word, who would perform "live" research and personalized, statistical analysis with respect to which style of preaching was to be the most effective way for proclaiming the gospel in the twenty-first century. This sermon research team proved to be most helpful with a matrix based on the following questions:

1. Which style most engages the hearers cognitively?
2. Which style enables memorization of the Word of the Lord?
3. Which style sustains application of that Word?

I was able to deliver four topical sermons to this particular team and receive strong statistical feedback. The first topical sermon I delivered was a sermon called, "The Crowd, the Christ, and a Desperate Touch." It was a part of our series titled "CSI" (Christ Scenes Investigated). The particular sermon and "scene" from Christ's life came from Luke 8:40–48. In this passage, Jesus was on his way to heal Jairus's daughter. During his travels, a woman who had been hemorrhaging for twelve years found her way to Christ in the crowd and touched the hem of his garment. The power of God pulsated through Jesus and healed this woman on the spot, even though she had spent all her money on local physicians never to be healed. Given the meaning of the text, I extrapolated a sermon topic of "desperate need of God; healing and faith needed in approaching Christ." This allowed me to apply the text to the congregation early on, stating, "You know, the last thing we really expect is God to fully break out in our midst and start doing things that only God can do! It is a frightening thing to be in the presence of God. And yet, that is exactly what we all want and that is what none of us really want."

That sermon topic then drove me to other scriptural passages. First, I addressed James 2:18, where the Bible says, "Show me your faith apart from your works, and I will show you my faith by my works" (ESV). Second, and because this particular sermon happened to fall on the second anniversary of 9/11, I was able to address Psalm 91:1 which says, "He who dwells in the shelter of the Most High will abide in the shadow of the Almighty" (ESV). Finally, the topic drove me to highlight Isaiah 40:29–31, which says, "He gives power to the faint, and to him who has no might he increases strength. Even youths shall faint and be weary, and young men shall fall exhausted; but they who wait for the LORD shall renew their strength; they shall mount up with wings like eagles; they shall run and not be weary; they shall walk and not faint" (ESV).

In the end, the sermon began with a specific passage, extrapolated the main topic of that particular passage to form a sermon topic, and then let that topic drive the rest of the sermon toward other biblical passages which naturally informed it. On a scale of one to four, with one being most topical and four being least topical, the sermon research team ranked this message third.

The second topical sermon I preached was entitled "The Marriage Matrix, Part III—Probing Beneath the Surface." This sermon began with a poignant scene from the movie *The Matrix*. From that scene, I reiterated a point that we had been making for some time in our church—that marriage is hard work. I pointed out how Mike Breaux, former teaching pastor at Willowcreek Community Church and now senior pastor at Heartland Community Church, discusses the way in which marriage, understood from a biblical worldview, involves two imperfect people diligently pursuing intimacy with one another through a committed relationship under the loving reign of God. Under this major theme, this sermon proceeded to discuss how vastly different men are from women, a key reason why marriage often feels like such hard work. From there, I then bounced around within Scripture, in classic, topical fashion, to discuss the nature and practice of marriage. I first took the congregation to Genesis 1:27 to show that God created males and females differently. Next I discussed the differences between men and women when it comes to verbal communication, emotional connection, nurturing affection, ultimate purpose, and secure confidence. Under each of these headings, a variety of Scripture passages were mentioned by way of support for the subtopic at hand. Given that the sermon topic of marriage determined the texts that were addressed (as opposed to a text determining the sermon topic), the lack of any one main text from which to base the sermon, and the springboarding style with which all passages were discussed, this was a classic topical sermon and as such ranked first within the topical rotation.

The third topical sermon brought us to the end of the year and the Christmas series titled "The Return of the King." The subtitle within this series was, "The Due Date Is Way Over Due," and the central text was Isaiah 9:1–7. The topic, as indicated by the title, was the Advent theme of waiting. I began the sermon by establishing the theme through a personal vignette of my children and their combination of excitement and dread at having to wait for Christmas to arrive. This sermon then turned to Isaiah 9:1–7 to discuss the way in which Israel kept waiting for the coming Messiah. They were hopeful, as Isaiah 9 demonstrates, but the wait was nonetheless difficult. I continued the waiting theme by then moving toward our own waiting and how Advent reminds us that we live in a precarious time between times. To further illustrate this point, I drew upon 1 Thessalonians 4:13—5:11, in which the apostle teaches the church about our waiting and Jesus' eventual return. By way of application and conclusion, I then posed the question, "What do we do as we wait?" This afforded me the opportunity to draw the congregation's attention back to the original Isaiah passage and its description of how God's character as a wonderful counselor, mighty God, Prince of Peace, and everlasting Father subsequently shapes how we live in relationship to him, while waiting for his return.

This particular topical sermon drove to a conclusion but not a lot of resolution. That is, it did not necessarily end with a problem solved, but it did remind us that one of our primary purposes, as we live in this time between the times, is to wait and wait faithfully. In fact the sermon ended rather inductively as I stated, "The due date was way overdue for the people of God, but God came and as a result we celebrate Christmas. But don't forget, God will come again. Until he comes, like Isaiah and the people of Israel, we do all we can to prepare others for his coming, and we wait!"

This sermon was topical but far more exegetical than most topical sermons, given that it did not stray much from the original passage in Isaiah 9 and drew its subject matter of waiting from the passage. As such, the sermon research team ranked this message fourth among the topical sermons preached for this research.

The fourth and final topical sermon in the rotation was from the series "High Five—Going to the Next Level!" The metaphor for this entire series was the human hand. The particular finger this message focused on was the pinky finger and how it is small but powerful. The use of this particular finger was a springboard from which I spoke about small groups, which are also small but powerful. Using true stories from the lives of people in our church, I spoke about how small groups have a powerful influence in our lives. For example, a young woman who was afraid to tell her parents about her faith in Christ because they said they would disown her if she became a Christian found Christ and authentic community. Then there was the small girl in our church who wept at night while her mother was passed out with a bottle in her hand. From those personal stories, I moved the congregation toward Mark 2:1–12 as a wonderful picture of a small group coming to the aid of man in need of healing by Jesus. In typical topical fashion, I then moved to Acts 2:46–47 to give a picture of the first-century church's tendency to meet in the context of small groups. This allowed me to make several key points of application: (1) biblical small groups are committed to hearing the Word; (2) biblical small groups are committed to experiencing forgiveness; and (3) biblical small groups are committed to experiencing healing. I concluded the message by giving an invitation to those who were not already connected in a small group to do so with one of the many groups already established within the church. Given all the above characteristics, this sermon ranked second on the list of topical sermons.

topical preaching test findings

Interestingly, the topical preaching style ranks highest among the three styles for its ability to engage and capture the attention of the listener. This means that the typical parishioner who grants a speaker twenty to forty minutes of time is most engaged when that speaker addresses a topic relating to real-life issues. If, as Craddock states, the goal of the preacher is not just to speak but also to earn a hearing, then speaking to relevant topics that engage the listener from the outset is a wise and effective choice.

However, it is important to note that even though the topical sermon engages the audience most, the data indicates that it is also the least effective in giving believers an ability to memorize the Word of the Lord. This lack of memorization is unfortunate since the engagement level is so high. This research is noteworthy because one's natural tendency is to assume the listener will memorize that in which he or she is most engaged. However, this is not the case. Even though listeners might very well remember the sermon topic or points of an outline, the topical style of bouncing through the Scriptures renders most listeners unable to remember any one passage for any length of time. This is an incredibly important finding if we want to help people memorize the Bible and thus develop a biblical worldview.

The topical style also did not score highest in the area of application. This could be due to the fact that many topical sermons are more concerned with substantiating the topic at hand than applying it to the audience. Thus, while topical sermons might very well engage the listener, given their relevance, they by and large leave a lot to be desired in one's ability to remember the

Word of the Lord and apply it to real-life situations. As such, the smart topical pastor will think of creative ways to help listeners memorize the Word and spend creative time offering real-life application.

The final predominant style that we have yet to discuss is narrative preaching. Indeed, this is fertile soil for delivering God's Word in the twenty-first century. As we will see, it is this style, I believe, that is most promising for connecting the dots and engaging listeners today. But before I get ahead of myself, we need to do our due diligence and closely examine narrative preaching just as we have done with the expository and topical styles.

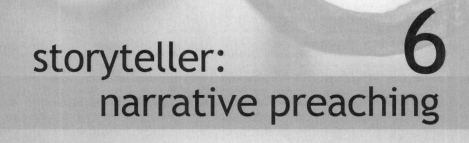

storyteller:
narrative preaching

6

Narrative is the telling of a story. In the case of narrative preaching, the story is the life-transforming, biblical and historical news of Jesus Christ's life, death, and resurrection that has given humanity the opportunity to be redeemed if accepted by faith. Narrative preaching, like expository and topical preaching, contains elements of both teaching and preaching. The teaching comes through the careful exegesis of the text, and the preaching is evident in the purpose toward which the narrative moves. That is, an effective narrative preacher inextricably interweaves story and sermon into one, seamless unit. Like traditional expository sermons, the authority of the narrative sermon is grounded firmly in the ancient texts of the Old and New Testaments. Yet like topical sermons, the narrative style is concerned with communicating those ancient texts in a relevant and personalized manner.

biblical precedents in narrative preaching

The roots of narrative preaching grow deep in the heart of the biblical Canon. In fact, of the three preaching styles, narrative preaching is the most biblically indigenous, since the texts of the Old and New Testaments are mostly narrative in the first place. Since the Bible is, by and large, one continuous storybook telling of God's unfailing love for his creation, those of us who love the Bible should, by default, value story.

Nearly forty years ago, H. Grady Davis reminded preachers to craft their sermons "in sync with the Bible," given that while only one-tenth of the gospel is exposition, nine-tenths of it is narrative.[1] The greatest advocate for narrative preaching therefore seems to be the Bible itself. The fact that the Bible is primarily narrative does more to develop a convincing case for storytelling preaching than any preacher could ever articulate.

Like the Bible, narrative sermons are not about loosely connected, cute stories, as some might suggest. Solid narrative preaching consists of earthy stories communicating the single overarching story of humankind being reconciled to God through the birth, life, death, and resurrection of Jesus Christ. That is, faithful narrative preaching creatively retells the biblical stories of faith, while employing the stories of individuals' lives in order to reveal God's incarnational presence among his people, the church.

the preacher as storyteller

The third and final preaching image is that of a storyteller. The storyteller image differs from the herald in that it describes the preacher not by his or her role, but by how the preacher exercises his or her role: telling stories. The storyteller image has received increasing attention within preaching literature, making the storytelling style increasingly popular in ministerial practice. Advocates of this image suggest that the storytelling preacher actually blends the best traits of the herald and the pastor without bringing along their most serious faults. Thomas Long elaborates on the nature of the storyteller image: "The storyteller . . . can be just as attuned to the biblical message as the herald and, at the same time, just as sensitive to the human situation as the pastor. What enables the preacher to combine these virtues is the use of narrative as the sermonic form of choice."[2]

The storyteller is a strong image because the Bible, when taken as a whole, can be described as a story; a vast, loosely structured, nonfiction novel, which, though containing many books, has one main plot about the love and truth of God that's given by grace through faith to a broken and hurting creation through the person and work of Jesus Christ his Son.

For the sake of clarification, it must be noted that when we speak of storyteller as an image, we are not talking about the use of a story within a sermon. That would be a narrative element (of which we will speak in a moment). Rather, the image of storyteller concerns not simply an element, but an entire style of preaching that begins in story format, is grounded in the redemptive, biblical narrative, and utilizes multiple stories throughout to communicate the central point of a given biblical passage. In this sense, the storyteller image characterizes the narrative preacher as a whole.

Jesus as the ultimate storyteller

One of the most fascinating aspects of Jesus that we encounter in the Bible is his uncanny ability to tell a great story. This was not just by happenstance either. Jesus made it clear that this form of communication was a strategy for ushering in the kingdom of God. I love how the impact of storytelling is described in Eugene Peterson's translation of the Bible, *The Message*. When the disciples asked Jesus why he told so many stories, he replied: "You've been given insight into God's kingdom. You know how it works. Not everybody has this gift, this insight; it hasn't been given to them. Whenever someone has a ready heart for this, the insights and understandings flow freely. But if there is no readiness, any trace of receptivity soon disappears. That's why I tell stories: to create readiness, to nudge the people toward receptive insight. In their present state they can stare till doomsday and not see it, listen till they're blue in the face and not get it" (Matt. 13:11–13 MSG).

Jesus was not only a great storyteller, but we find him often framing his entire message in narrative form. Jesus' parables are perfect examples of narrative preaching. Simon J. Kistemaker says, "All in all, the parables of Jesus were in a category all their own and were quite distinct from other parabolic teachings in their timelessness and universality. . . . Throughout the centuries they have addressed and continue to address people of all ages, nationalities, and races. In their crispness, they sparkle; they are novel, pertinent, and always exhibit inherent power."[3]

Take, for example, the parable of the prodigal son, or maybe it would be better titled prodigal *sons*. It's a classic story that has the ability to relate to every possible person in an audience. Whether we are of a more secular and irreligious nature like the younger son or of more a moralistic and religious bent like the older son, we all find ourselves playing a role in the story. After all, we are all either religious or irreligious and in need of grace from our heavenly Father. For years, storytellers have attempted to craft narratives that appeal to and connect with entire crowds, but never has anyone been quite so effective as Jesus.

extra-canonical precedents in narrative preaching

Over the years, three of the most avid advocates for narrative preaching have been Fred Craddock, William Willimon, and

Eugene Lowry. These storytellers have unapologetically said that preachers must rid themselves of many of their cherished norms for sermon preparation and delivery. The reason is because narrative preaching is not about stringing together similar stories or illustrations. Rather, the real heart of narrative preaching is inextricably connected to plot. Lowry says it this way, "First, we have to lay aside—at least temporarily—many of the cherished norms about sermon anatomy. . . . We need to also form a new image of the sermon . . . an *event-in-time*, a narrative art form more akin to a play or novel in shape than to a book. . . . We are narrative artists. . . . I propose that we begin by regarding the sermon as a homiletical plot, a narrative art form, a sacred story."[4]

According to Lowry, the driving force of effective narrative preaching is plot. He shapes his book, *The Homiletical Plot*, around two plot forms: the movie plot and the television series plot. The movie plot begins with a felt discrepancy and moves to an unknown resolution. The television series plot begins with a felt discrepancy and moves toward a known conclusion. He writes, "In whatever type of narrative plot, the event of the story moves from a bind, a felt discrepancy, an itch born of ambiguity, and moves toward the solution."[5] In short, a narrative sermon is any sermon arranged in such a way that all ideas, stories, and illustrations strategically delay the unveiling of the sermon's meaning.

Given this, narrative preaching is closely related to what is known as inductive preaching because inductive preaching derives its name from a "particular" to a "general" movement of ideas. This, of course, stands in stark contrast to deductive preaching, which moves from the general to the particular. Narrative preaching, like the expository and topical styles, has incredible strengths for proclaiming the Word of the Lord and notable weaknesses. It is to the strengths that we now turn.

strengths of narrative preaching

The word *story*, which is synonymous with narrative preaching, has been a buzzword of late within the academy of biblical preaching. Everyone has a story, and if the gospel story somehow unites individuals' stories together in a grand, redemptive narrative, the question now becomes: How do preachers seamlessly proclaim that gospel story in such a way that it intersects with their hearers' stories? Answering this question is not an easy task. In fact, effective and faithful narrative preaching is hard work, but when done correctly and under the anointing of the Holy Spirit, the strengths are astonishing.

As David Buttrick says, "Jesus came preaching."[6] While he could have come singing or writing books, he chose to come preaching. This preaching, I might add, was mostly narrative in nature. One of the most obvious strengths of narrative preaching, therefore, is that it correctly considers the predominant narrative genre of the Bible. As stated earlier, over 90 percent of the Bible is narrative. This fact might seem incidental to critics, but we must take heed to consider the genre and form of the Bible we preach. An inherent strength is brought to the preaching process when the style of the sermon is commensurate at best, and tangentially related at worst, with how Jesus proclaimed the kingdom of God and how the Bible itself is structured. In other words, the storyteller's message is not only to be shaped by personal stories or even the stories of Jesus, but also the embodiment of God's reign as patterned by Jesus. In this sense, the narrative sermon is, to some degree, a performance of Scripture, which gives urgency and importance to how one structures a sermon, not merely how one decorates it.

Another major strength of storytelling preaching is the engagement it creates with the listeners. Every wise preacher knows that the task of preaching is not only speaking the truth, but also making sure the truth is rightly heard by the listener. In a real sense, what is heard is as important as what is said. Nothing, I believe, creates tension, interest, and engagement more effectively than a story or, in this case, a sermon structured around story.

In researching four narrative preachers, I was able to read over twenty outstanding narrative sermons. By far, two of the best narrative sermons I have ever experienced, "The Second Sin" and "Jonah's Christmas Story," were preached by Dr. J. Ellsworth Kalas of Asbury Theological Seminary.[7] "The Second Sin," is by far one of the most well-crafted and insightful sermons on Genesis 3:1–3. Kalas approached the text from a unique angle. Rather than preaching on Adam and Eve's first sin of disobedience, Kalas uncovered humanity's second sin: the attempt to cover sin with excuses. After he caused the hearer to squirm with curiosity as to what the second sin is, he made a note:

> Adam answered, "Yes, but it was the woman you gave me who brought me some, and I ate it." And Eve not to be left bearing sole responsibility, chimed in, "The serpent tricked me." Now there you have the second sin. It is even more dangerous than the first, because it prevents our recovering from the first. It is the sin of *excuses*—the unwillingness to admit that we are wrong and the refusal to see ourselves for what we are. . . . When we become guilty of the second sin, the sin of excusing ourselves and of being unwilling to face ourselves, we close the door against God and hope.[8]

Since the Bible reminds us in Romans 3:23 that all have sinned and fallen short of the glory of God, I loved the theological richness of this sermon. Since all are bound to sin, one would think we know that any form of pride or pretentious sinlessness cannot save us. Moreover, since we receive the grace of God by humbly declaring our sinfulness and need for a Savior, the fact that the sin of excuse-making pride is at least as deadly as the first sin makes remarkable sense. I found this theological point to be somewhat like an epiphany, as I had never consciously considered the deadliness of the second sin. This kind of curious tension and unfolding of the plot is one of the great strengths of well-crafted narrative sermons. When done well, the sermon fully engages listeners and has them on the edge of their seats anticipating some form of gospel resolution.

Kalas's second sermon, entitled "Jonah's Christmas Story," was equally fascinating and well written. The two biblical texts from which the sermon was drawn were Jonah 3:1–6, 10 and Matthew 12:38–42. The sermon began by recalling that infamous *A Christmas Carol* villain known as Scrooge. The preacher immediately juxtaposed Scrooge with Jonah saying, "And before you write me off by muttering, 'Jonah's a fish story, not a Christmas story,' I ask you to hear me out. When I'm done, perhaps you'll agree that . . . Jonah himself was the original, archetypal Scrooge."[9]

Kalas proceeded to retell the popular story of Jonah while juxtaposing it with the Christmas story, until it climaxed with the following statement: "But see the proportions of the

Christmas story. Jonah was called to preach to his enemies; Jesus was asked to *die* for them. Jonah was unwilling to go until he was forced to do so; Jesus said, 'My food is to do the will of him who sent me' (John 4:34). Jonah spent three days in the belly of a great fish because he was running from God. Jesus spent three days in the belly of the earth because he was running *for* God.'"[10]

Kalas is at his best when he is telling and retelling the biblical story with rich and illustrative mastery over the English language, while maintaining a staunch faithfulness to the Word of God. Like a great Broadway show or Hollywood blockbuster, a well-crafted narrative sermon keeps you engaged from start to finish. Few, if any, do this better than Ellsworth Kalas.

A third strength of the narrative sermon is movement. As we see in Kalas's narrative sermons, a great amount of movement is utilized: movement from problem to resolution, plot introduction to climax and conclusion, and more. The result is not only that the listener is engaged, but when done properly, the listener is moved from a sense of his or her own sinfulness and brokenness to the cross of Christ and his resurrection, and a deeper appreciation and faith in both.

The final strength of narrative preaching is related to effective communication. That is, narrative preaching is not simply a cutesy way of promoting stories. Rather, the case for storytelling can be made in a sophisticated manner based on what listeners usually like and remember the most about sermons: the stories. I have yet to find anyone who would deny that they like stories. Not only do individuals like stories, but people live through and interpret their lives out of them. They remember in stories, dream in stories, and shape their values through stories. Long after Sunday dinner, when the rest of the sermon is forgotten, listeners still recall the stories told. In like fashion, the Bible says that Jesus "did not speak to them without a parable" (Mark 4:34 ESV). "Given the power of narration," writes Buttrick, "is it surprising that through most of the Christian centuries preaching has been discursive, [that is to say] best described as storytelling?"[11]

A fitting example is the phrase, "Once upon a time." For many, these words conjure up memories of past stories from childhood. For others, this phrase transports them to lands of make believe. The words are like a giant spotlight that invades the darkness and illumines the stage before the actors even arrive. In fact, this phrase creates expectation and prepares the listener for a story. "Every sermon," says Roger Van Harn, "needs the spirit if not the letters of those words."[12] Narrative preaching enables the listener to understand his or her story in the awesome light of God's story. When experiencing narrative proclamation of the Word, God's people are encouraged to reexamine their stories under the penetrating power of God's story behind each and every biblical text. When done effectively, it is a great strength of narrative preaching. However, as with the other preaching styles, there are weaknesses that must be acknowledged and addressed.

weaknesses of narrative preaching

In the midst of growing vitality in the area of homiletics and particularly narrative preaching, Charles Campbell notes that beneath the surface are signs of trouble.[13] Unfortunately, the new preaching theories and resources do not appear to have brought new life to the church. Over the same period that storytelling preaching has enjoyed resurgence, mainline Protestant churches have been in decline. Obviously, something has been lacking in preaching. Preachers in search of the Promised Land have tried inductive preaching, story preaching, dialogue sermons, and homiletical plots. While these new methods have been exciting for the moment, many preachers sense something is missing. Preachers have wandered amid the myriad of books, articles, and continuing education conferences; but still have not found what they are looking for, possibly attesting to the fact that the problem does not lie merely in external form. The idea that something may yet be missing in the pulpit of Jesus' church, something that cannot be answered by external form, deserves further investigation.

While this method of preaching, in the hands of a faithful and effective storyteller, has immense potential and power in proclaiming the Word of the Lord, in the wrong hands, it has devastating potential for the church. First, narrative preaching, which is at its heart "gospel storytelling," can easily become "my storytelling." Little distance exists between telling my story as opposed to telling the gospel story, and unfortunately, many preachers have crossed over to the other side. Søren Kierkegaard most often took the heat for dangerously and delicately balancing between the two sides of the story. As Craddock rightly notes, "The writings of Kierkegaard became the scholarly footnote legitimizing the transformation of theology into autobiography."[14] This autobiographical tendency becomes a travesty when one again considers the individualism so prevalent in the Western world today.

When I become consumed with my story, preaching the gospel story becomes increasingly difficult. Moreover, even with the noblest attempts, times arise in which we begin to interpret and therefore preach God's story through the prism of our stories, which amputates the fullness of the gospel and forces us into a myopic view of God, his grandeur, and his plan for human history. We can quickly make God into our own image, forgetting that he was the one who created us. If we are not careful, the subject of our worship becomes not the God of the Bible but our personal projections of God seen and interpreted through the lens of personal story. As a consequence, Jesus gets absorbed into human experiences and the church loses the unique and irreplaceable identity of Jesus. The problem with personal projections is that we Christians do not worship a particular genre or creation of God, but rather the one whose identity is irreplaceable and rendered through the biblical story of Jesus. This is a caution of epic proportions for the narrative, storytelling preachers among us.

A second weakness of narrative preaching, but not isolated only to narrative preaching, is the liberal theological elevation of the role of individual experience in the proclamation of the gospel. Liberal theology has basically sought to correlate the Christian message with dimensions of human experience that can be discerned apart from Jesus and the Christian faith itself. Once these experiences have been discerned, the Christian message is made meaningful for modern people by being expressed in terms of those independently discovered human needs and experiences. Craddock makes a claim regarding this preaching process: "Experience figures prominently in the process [of narrative preaching], not just at the point of *receiving* lessons and truths to be implemented, but in the process of *arriving* at those truths. . . . It cannot be overemphasized that the immediate and concrete experiences of the people are significant ingredients in the formation and movement of the sermon and not simply the point at which final applications and exhortations are joined."[15]

Granted, the experiences of the preacher and the listeners are crucial and common points for understanding the gospel. However, a weakness exists when personal experience becomes paramount in the entire process of interpreting the gospel, particularly when personal experience is enamored by and in the grip of a culture that promotes radical individualism and the pluralism we spoke about in chapter 2. The result is that the preaching can become nothing more than "warmed over" religious platitudes held loosely together by imagination, cute stories, and human need. After experiencing this kind of assault on narrative preaching, one is left wondering if Jesus' incarnation and subsequent death, burial, and resurrection are even needed to support this kind of preaching. Rather, Jesus becomes little more than a cipher for an independent understanding of human existence—a human existence, of course, that sets the terms and parameters for living. In other words, from a theological perspective, Christology becomes a function of anthropology. An analysis of the human situation and all the experiences therein shape the church's understanding of Jesus rather than the other way around. The results are incredibly dangerous to the life of the church and those who want to follow Jesus.

A perfect example of this homiletical disaster is found in one of the most well-known sermons of the twentieth century, Paul Tillich's "You Are Accepted."[16] Tillich's work serves as an appropriate illustration of the dangers of liberalism and narrative preaching run amuck. Tillich's aim is to make the Christian message meaningful by relating it to the general human experience that it expresses. In his sermon, Jesus has no unique, irreplaceable identity. At best, his presence is diffused throughout general human experience. Indeed, the only mention of Christ occurs in relation to Paul's experience and acceptance of him on the Damascus road, at Paul's moment of greatest separation from other people, himself, and God. In "You Are Accepted," Jesus Christ practically disappears and plays little to no role in humanity's acceptance. As one can imagine, the implications of this kind of radical liberal theology for preaching are extraordinarily frightful. After all, the only reason man can be acceptable is because of Jesus' life, sacrificial death, and glorious resurrection.

A final weakness of narrative preaching can be summed up in the fact that this form of sermon preparation is just plain hard. Of all the preaching styles discussed in this project, I have concluded that narrative preaching, which can be exegetically faithful, is a difficult art. To craft a sermon which is true to the biblical text and also excellent as a storytelling presentation of the gospel is no easy feat. Far easier, in my opinion, is the herald's task of staying within a text expositionally or bouncing back and forth throughout Scripture as a pastor with a relevant topic than it is for the storytelling preacher to craft a narrative sermon with all of its complexities, nuances, and plot movement. After all, is it not easier to explain a film or have a conversation about film topics than it is to craft a screenplay? However, the work required for narrative sermons should not keep preachers from utilizing this style, but in light of the relative demands on a preacher's time, the difficulty of crafting narrative sermons must be considered a weakness.

testing the strengths and weaknesses of narrative preaching

The first narrative sermon I preached to the new**hope** church family and the sermon research team for evaluation and statistical analysis was part of an August 2003 sermon series on joy. The sermon was grounded in Philippians 3:1–16 and titled "Finding Joy in All the Wrong Places." It was narrative to its core as I wove stories together in a multilayered fashion, all the while narrating the biblical truths behind Philippians 3:1–16. The sermon was rich in story and illustration but only insofar as each was taken from the primary passage of Philippians 3:12–14. Those verses state, "I press on to take hold of that for which Christ Jesus took hold of me. Brothers, I do not consider myself yet to have taken hold of it. But one thing I do: Forgetting what is behind and straining toward what is ahead, I press on toward the goal to win the prize for which God has called me heavenward in Christ Jesus."

Eventually, I moved the sermon to a point of invitation and invited the congregation to fully surrender and commit to Christ. In that vein and because the apostle Paul wrote his letter from a jail cell and referred to himself as a slave or servant of Christ Jesus, I had hundreds of chain links scattered throughout the congregation. As part of the invitation, I simply asked people to commit their lives to Christ and acknowledge that commitment by getting out of their seats to pick up a chain link. I pointed out that in order to pick up a chain link, one had to kneel down. The Spirit of God moved as our worship arts ministry led our congregation in the song "I Surrender." The service concluded with hundreds of people on their knees, with a chain link in their hand singing, "I surrender all." It was a moving experience. On a scale of one to four, with one being most narrative and four being least narrative, the sermon research team ranked this message second.

The second narrative sermon I preached was titled "The Marriage Matrix, Part I." This sermon would not be true to the style of narrative, however, as I felt compelled to actually introduce marriage in a broad-stroke fashion. As such, the sermon felt much more topical than narrative. Ultimately, the sermon was well received and meaningful for the church, but not as a narrative sermon. On a scale of one to four, therefore, this sermon ranked fourth in the narrative category.

The third narrative sermon was delivered on Thanksgiving weekend and aptly titled "Thanksgiving." The sermon derived itself from Psalm 30 and began in a storytelling fashion, discussing Thanksgiving and the beauty of this holiday. I said, "There is nothing like giving thanks for what we receive. And this holiday is one of the most beautiful of the year, in my opinion. There is nothing expected in return, just giving thanks." Since a truly narrative sermon is interconnected with Scripture and stories, I walked the congregation through Psalm 30, weaving stories as I went. Hopefully, it was done seamlessly enough that the congregation was often unaware of where Scripture began and ended. After leading the congregation through the first ten verses of the passage, the sermon took a turn and moved the congregation from a faithful understanding of suffering in the world to celebration, as God turns our wailing into dancing (Ps. 30:11–12). Finally, the sermon concluded with a story about George Thomas, a pastor in a small New England town who, for a mere ten dollars, purchased a bird cage and three little birds that were shivering with cold and fright from a boy desiring only to trap and kill the birds. Narratively, the parallel was then drawn to the imagery of Satan wanting only to trap and kill us, but Jesus giving not merely ten dollars, but his entire life in order to save us. I finished by simply asking, "What are you thankful for?" The sermon research team ranked this message first among the narrative sermons.

The fourth narrative sermon in the rotation was from a series entitled "High Five—Going to the Next Level!" As mentioned previously, this was a series that used the hand as a teaching metaphor. Each finger represented a topic or point made in the message. This particular sermon was grounded in John 4:5–42 and was subtitled "Pointing the Way," with the index finger being the digit in focus. As I progressed through the story of John 4, I drew out the following points:

- Become a friend (John 4:7).
- Be ready to share the good news (John 4:13–14).
- Don't let people get you off target (John 4:20).
- Observe God's power at work (John 4:39).

Each of these points was narratively discussed from the passage and in conjunction with culturally relevant stories. At the end of the sermon, I integrated the old familiar illustration using the hands to represent the church and the steeple. I said, "Here is the church and here is the steeple, open the door and here are all the people." But after a pause said, "No, I don't think that is exactly right. Here is the church, here is the steeple, open the door, and release all the people," at which point I connected the text to the vision of our church which is to reach, teach and release. After all, Jesus' encounter with the Samaritan woman at the well was and is a great opportunity to craft a narrative sermon that communicates to the church our need to cross cultural boundaries and build redemptive relationships with people who are different and sometimes far from God. On a scale of one to four, this sermon ranked third.

narrative preaching test findings

After evaluating the four narrative sermons in conjunction with the topical and expository sermons, I was able to draw some interesting and final conclusions. As mentioned in chapter 5, what I found throughout all of the sermons was that the topical style of preaching was statistically more engaging than either the expository or narrative styles. However, the narrative style of preaching came in a close second. This finding seemed consistent with how we typically function. We love to be entertained by stories. Therefore, when a preacher tells stories that not only entertain, but also connect listeners to the gospel of Jesus Christ, people's eyes open wide and their bodies lean forward. Simply put, you have both the power of God's Word and the appeal of the story working on your side.

Negatively, in relation to one's ability to memorize the Word of the Lord, the data reveals that narrative sermons are not the best. They were certainly not as good as expository sermons for helping people memorize scriptural texts. They were, however, slightly more effective than topical sermons, given how narrative elements can captivate a person to the extent that they more readily recall the biblical text that was being narrated.

On a more positive note, the narrative sermon ranked higher than either the expository or topical styles for life application. According to statistical analysis, three of the four highest life application scores from the twelve sermons preached for this project came from narrative sermons. The implication is that a believer is most likely to change behavior after listening to a message they enjoy and that captures their attention through story. This is an extremely important point to remember and should greatly impact the effort we put into making our church services and messages enjoyable. And for the record, enjoyable and challenging are by no means mutually exclusive, especially when it comes to preaching.

We have briefly touched on the history of expository, topical, and narrative sermons; identified corresponding images associated with each type; identified major strengths and weaknesses; and looked at which style most effectively engages the listener, enabling him or her to memorize the Word, and actually applying that for authentic life change. Now it is time to start moving toward an applicable conclusion for those desiring to more faithfully and effectively preach the Word of the Lord in the twenty-first century.

connecting
the dots

7

Up until this point, I have tried to present an unbiased view of the three most common styles of Christian preaching. In doing so, I have shared a process by which a sermon research team and I went about studying the effectiveness and faithfulness of each style in a postmodern context. I have intentionally tried to keep my cards close to my chest so that together we could experience and explore the faithfulness and effectiveness of expository, narrative, and topical preaching. However, it is time for me to lay down my hand to hopefully persuade you to try and integrate narrative *elements* into your proclamation of the gospel, regardless of whether you choose to cultivate an overall expository, narrative, or topical *style* of preaching.

In light of the current need for and dilemma surrounding faithful and effective biblical preaching, I must state that it has never been the goal of this book to recreate the preaching wheel by proposing some kind of fourth style apart from expository, narrative, or topical preaching. Nor do I want to advocate on the side of any one particular style and thereby throw more fuel onto the preaching predicament fire. Rather, my goal from this point forward is to demonstrate that each style of preaching can be both equally faithful to the biblical text, and effective at reaching postmodern people if consideration is given toward integrating narrative elements, or what I will call "storyness," into the sermon.

Storyness encompasses the idea that people learn best and are subsequently changed the most when they are shown as well as told. The child learns how to act not simply from what the parent says, but also by observing the parent. As a father of five, I can assure you that my children learn far more from what they observe in the story of my life than what I say to each of them. If you have children, be assured the same is true for you. This is bigger than a parent-child relationship as well. The employee learns what is acceptable in the workplace not simply through an HR manual, but by observing the behaviors of fellow coworkers. More specifically, the businessman or woman grows to become generous by beholding the beauty of generosity and the ugliness of greed, rather than simply being told he or she needs to be less greedy. Charles Dickens's classic story *A Christmas Carol* taught us that. We learn and are changed by seeing in conjunction with hearing, by being shown while also being told. We learn through verbal storyness, those narrative elements that show as well as tell.

Storyness, however, is not simply an issue of practicality. It is uniquely biblical as well. It is grounded in the idea that the Bible is not only meant to be heard, but also beheld, embodied, and lived. The word that pierces "to the division of soul and of spirit" (Heb. 4:12 ESV) is a word that is not only verbal but entirely personal in the incarnation of Jesus Christ. It is why the gospel writer John was able to say that the "Word [meaning Jesus] was with God, and the Word was God" (John 1:1). The word is not only the verbal message of Jesus, but the person of Jesus as well. One might say that storyness, then, was an essential part of Jesus as a person.

Furthermore, storyness is why Jesus taught in parables more than any other form of communication in the Gospels—an estimated one-third of the time. Parables allowed Jesus to show his listeners the meaning behind his message rather than just tell it to them. With parables, Jesus was able to communicate a deep truth through real-world pictures and circumstances.

Storyness is also why we so often see Jesus acting out the gospel in the Bible. Take for example, the time when he bent down to the level of the woman caught in adultery and wrote in the dirt (John 8:3–11). He was showing her with his actions and words that he was her advocate. And how much more powerful must it have been to that broken and shamed woman to see the Savior of the world bend down in love rather than just hear that he loved her.

On another level, one could even say that storyness was the foundation for how Jesus and the apostles taught kingdom truths. For example, Jesus stated that he came to give abundant life (John 10:10). Notice that he did not say that he came to give nifty teachings or winsome lessons. Jesus was concerned with showing and telling truth in such a way that it would play out in people's lives as opposed to remaining merely cognitive. Similarly, the apostle Peter stated that Jesus' "divine power has granted to us all things that pertain to life and godliness" (2 Pet. 1:3 ESV). Notice that he did not say that "Jesus' divine power has granted to us all things that pertain to religious lessons and curriculums." Like Jesus, Peter understood that the gospel was something to be lived throughout every facet of our lives, and so merely telling it without showing it would do an injustice to its very nature. Finally, the apostle Paul exhorted fellow Christians to "work out your own salvation with fear and trembling" (Phil. 2:12 ESV). His language was rife with telling and showing. Notice he did not say, "Dwell pensively on your salvation." The gospel is meant to be embodied and lived after heard and believed. All of this is to say that when we incorporate storyness into our sermons, we not only follow in the tradition of Peter, Paul, and ultimately Jesus, but we help our people behold the truth of the gospel in such a way that they are given greater opportunity to be transformed by its beauty.

As a preacher, I have learned to deal with the fact that people will not always remember what I say or do. However, I have come to believe that they will almost always remember how I make them feel. Stories make people feel. The feelings might be good, bad, or sad, but there is no denying that it is through stories that we connect and feel deeply.

Recently, my wife and I were having what I will term a "discussion" around the kitchen table. A more apt word would be *fight*, but it certainly did not start out that way. Thankfully, the kids were already in bed, which granted us greater freedom for expression. As we discussed the topic, we both began to grow increasingly agitated. I realized that my wife did not understand the points that were being communicated (in my opinion) with the utmost eloquence and logic. After all, I'm a preacher with the spiritual gift of gab. In my mind, what I was saying made perfect sense and Amy Lynn's sinful nature was keeping her from understanding my verbal perfection. Yet all my wife was hearing from me was a certain, condescending tone of voice. Nearing the brink of a verbal apocalypse, my wife paused and simply said to me, "Can you bring your voice down? It's not what you are saying that is bothering me, but how you are saying it!" While everything I said to my wife might have been correct, that wasn't the point. She understood a deeper truth: that my actions—in this case my tone of voice and body language—were speaking louder than my words.

What I was showing her was different than what I was telling her, and frankly, my storyness or lack thereof was clouding my message. The same goes for those of us who preach and teach the Bible. The message we have is of the utmost importance and therefore ought to be storied in the best way possible, lest we cloud out the life-transforming message of the gospel.

So whether you consider yourself a staunch proponent of a strictly expository method, a creative and relevant topical preacher, a captivating storyteller, or simply an aspiring preacher or teacher of the Bible, my prayer is that in learning how to incorporate storyness into your sermons and teachings, you will be able connect the dots between the gospel, the relativistic society in which we live, and the hearers who have entrusted you to bring forth the Word of the Lord. In doing so, I believe you will become a more powerful and effective preacher. And as a more effective preacher, you will have a greater capacity to help people from all walks of life love Jesus, both for their blessing and his glorious advancement of the kingdom.

The beauty and power of integrating narrative elements into our preaching is that it speaks the language of those in our relativistic culture and affirms the witness and authority of Scripture. This is because narrative elements make the Bible and gospel personal. As mentioned previously, it has become common in our postmodern culture, whether religious or irreligious, to denounce objective truth and any overarching story that claims to make sense of the world in favor of subjective truthiness grounded only in personal feelings and experiences. Thus, the Bible and the Christian faith are easily rejected. The problem, however, is that without an overarching story by which to understand life and the world, our own personal stories and lives become confusing, isolated, and insignificant. Author Richard Weaver says, "It has been well said that the chief trouble with the contemporary generation is that it has not read the minutes of the last meeting. . . . [This generation] is being starved for value. We are being told bigger lies and we are being fed less—this is the substantial fact flowing from the degradation of the ideal."[1]

The ideal of which Weaver speaks is the idea of an overarching story. Weaver continues by describing how a lack of ideal or overarching story ultimately destroys our ability to understand the world around us and properly operate within it: "It is naturally impossible for anyone to get along without some knowledge that he feels can be relied on. Having been told by the relativists that he cannot have truth, he now has 'facts.' Thus the acquisition of unrelated details becomes an end in itself and takes the place of the true ideal of education."[2]

One can only imagine the neurosis that would begin to form in our minds and hearts apart from an explanatory and revelatory overarching story. Depression, anxiety, suicidal tendencies, personality disorders, and obsessions have become all too common. After all, without a meta-narrative that overrides and connects all our stories together, our lives mean nothing, have little to no purpose, and are going nowhere—or at least nowhere that we understand. Incidentally, this is the reason why I do not think it is mere happenstance that major depression is one of the most common psychological disorders in the Western world.[3]

It is clear in my experience, and the data gathered from the new**hope** sermon research team strongly confirms that narrative elements are by far the most engaging and applicable for significant life change. Times have changed and so must our preaching. The gospel message of Jesus never changes but the method by which we communicate that message quite often has to change.

Without the engagement of story and the insatiable and overwhelming interest we find today for an overarching meta-narrative that can somehow make sense of my smaller story, the church is on the verge of losing a golden opportunity to witness a harvest of epic proportions. I still believe that the harvest is plentiful and that Christ still wants to send workers into the harvest field (Matt. 9:37). Could it be that part of our success, or lack thereof, in becoming eyewitnesses to this great and eternal harvest has much to do with how we actually communicate the gospel? I believe the answer to that question is yes and that the integration of narrative elements into our preaching, regardless of what style we use, is of paramount importance in that harvest.

Through the incorporation of narrative elements in our gospel presentations, we have the privilege of showing as opposed to merely telling the gospel, thus exposing its natural power all the more. After all, as we show the gospel, we draw people into the grand narrative of Scripture, showing them how their lives fit into the biblical story of creation, the fall, redemption, and restoration. The result is that our people are given a framework with which to understand the world around them and their lives within it. That is precisely what happened to my good friend Teresa, whom I introduced in chapter 2. When the cancer came, she was able to navigate this atrocious storm from a rock solid, biblical, narrative framework and not some shallow, weak, relativistic notion that all truths are equal and one story is no greater than the other. In a very real sense, the power and engagement of that story changed and saved her life!

By integrating narrative elements into the three main preaching styles discussed thus far, our people are given the purpose, acceptance, and significance they were created to know and crave. The power of the meta-narrative is that it connects the dots and links our various and sundry stories to God's story. Putting it bluntly, if we don't integrate narrative elements into our preaching, we might very well teach pure biblical messages but in the process find ourselves only preaching to the most committed and already saved, as opposed to having the unbelievable privilege of teaching a not-yet-convinced, pre-Christian crowd, where first-time conversions to Christ and believer baptisms actually become the norm and not the exception.

We might even say that when we integrate narrative elements into our preaching, we speak the gospel with storyness and begin to speak the love language, or native tongue, of humanity. Western humanity, being devoid of an overarching story to make sense of its own personal stories, especially craves such a narrative. When we use narrative elements to present truth in a culture that no longer values absolute truth, we share the common language of story that speaks to the deepest level of people's hearts and minds, thereby creating receptivity to the ultimate good news story of Jesus.

Incidentally, if storying the gospel speaks to the hearts of our people who are craving an overarching truth by which to make sense of their lives amidst a relativistic culture, then not storying the gospel would be incredibly unloving. If we know that our people, by default, crave and yearn for meaning, which is tied to the biblical narrative, it would be unloving if we fill our times of teaching and preaching with jokes, pithy anecdotes, and personal opinions as opposed to a verbal picture of the gospel story and its implications for giving meaning to each of our individual stories. After all, the good news that, as believers, we are forgiven and perfectly loved by God the Father because of the saving work of Christ (not because of any merit of our own) is the greatest news that any of us could ever want to hear. It is this overarching story that we all long to hear whether we know it or not. For in it the height, width, and breadth of divine beauty is displayed!

If we are going to be faithful to the biblical narrative and engaging and loving toward those in our relativistic culture, then we must be committed to a type of biblical preaching that makes use of narrative elements or storyness. It is well worth exploring how to use storyness in a way that upholds the truth of the Bible while affording us the opportunity to speak into a variety of urban and rural contexts.

narrative elements **8**
in urban and
rural settings

After all this talk about contextualization, you may still be thinking that while it makes sense that storyness and incorporating narrative elements into preaching would make a sermon more faithful and effective in a variety of contexts, your specific context is so unique that it wouldn't work for you. I agree! Narrative preaching may not be the best for your particular context. Remember that we are not talking about one style of preaching, but about incorporating narrative elements into any style of preaching. So before you throw this book to the wayside, let me share with you more about the context of my church in hopes of drawing out some universal principles for using storyness no matter the context.

Before I started new**hope** church in 2002 and prior to my doctoral studies at Asbury Theological Seminary, I pastored a small country church near Saxapahaw, North Carolina. Now, if you are thinking to yourself, "I have never heard of Saxapahaw,

North Carolina," neither had I; and you may never hear of it again. It literally has one yellow flashing light that sits atop a hill, overlooking the Haw River.

Amy Lynn and I loved serving the people of Salem Church. Salem comes from the word *shalom*, meaning "peace," and that is exactly what we experienced for three years while serving this rural congregation. When we arrived in 1997, this little community of faith was averaging around sixty people on a good Sunday. When we left for Asbury Seminary three kids and three years later, the church was maxing out both the building and parking lot with over 220 people. We built playgrounds, paved parking lots, put on the best fall festivals in the Carolinas, and saw regular attenders invite their pre-Christian friends and neighbors. And most importantly, we witnessed dozens of salvations and adult believer baptisms! God deserves the praise for these spiritual blessings (see Eph. 1:3).

Several years later, after returning from Kentucky, we launched new**hope** church in our home with those same three children. In ten years, God has opened the floodgates of heaven and multiplied this church plant from the Kelley family of five to over five thousand people who consider this their community of faith. I have often been asked how my preaching has changed from the days of teaching hundreds at Salem to now teaching over five thousand people at new**hope**. My answer has always been the same: "Nothing has really changed." Sure,

I hope I've matured as a communicator and grown in my leadership, but my preaching style hasn't really changed that much in the last decade. In fact, during those really crazy and busy weeks, I have been known to recycle a sermon from my days at Salem Church and preach it to the community of new**hope**.

Why has my preaching style not changed from an extremely rural setting of Salem to the suburban setting of new**hope**, you might ask? The answer is primarily that I believe the value of narrative elements in preaching is universal and transferrable, regardless of where one is serving. That is, the power of narrative elements in the preaching of God's Word, the engagement, ability to memorize, and life application, is timeless in effectiveness and universal in scope. If you're not convinced by my personal experience, maybe some demographic data and biblical examples will help.

According to Percept National Demographics and the U.S. Census Bureau, central North Carolina is an eclectic conglomeration of suburban and rural influences.[1] Let me explain.

Racially, the context is only moderately diverse. In the last decade, the white population was projected to increase slightly in number but decrease from 82.6 percent to 80.0 percent of the total population. The African-American population, on the other hand, was projected to increase from 8.3 percent to 8.7 percent of the total. The Hispanic/Latino population was projected to increase from 3.3 percent to 4.4 percent, while the Asian/other population was projected to increase from 5.8 percent to 7.0 percent of the total population.[2]

Economically, Chapel Hill is an extremely affluent area with the average household income being $82,830 a year, as compared to the national average of $56,184. Year after year, this area is ranked among the top places to live in the country by magazines and newspapers such as *Newsweek* and *USA Today*.

Educationally, the "young and coming" is the most populous group at 351.9 percent higher than the United States average. This demographic possesses a college graduation rate 157.6 percent higher than the national average, and a postgraduate degree rate 378.2 percent higher than the same national average.[3] Since Raleigh, Durham, Chapel Hill, and surrounding areas are university towns, the educational level of its people is extremely high. Nestled in the rolling hills of the Piedmont area, central North Carolina is the home of North Carolina State, North Carolina Central, Duke University, and the University of North Carolina. In other words, this area is the higher education mecca of North Carolina, and the people of this area pride themselves on their affection for academia.

The population growth and high level of education all contribute to one of the most important demographic indicators related to this particular study: worship preferences among the residents of Chapel Hill. As might be expected, those living in

Chapel Hill prefer "intellectually challenging" sermons. In fact, they prefer intellectually challenging sermons at a rate 77 percent higher than the national average.[4]

Though these demographics stem from a particular ministry context, they are also a reflection of a broader contextual issue: that a location can bear both urban and suburban/rural characteristics. For example, the racial makeup of central North Carolina in many ways reflects the homogeneity of a rural town, while the educational makeup reflects the high academic levels of many of our country's leading urban centers. Situated somewhere between the economic makeup of this area as a whole is the suburban area. As such, central North Carolina is the quintessential "urbal" community or community possessing urban, suburban, and rural elements. This means that to be effective here, ministry must have elements that can be effective in predominately rural, urban, and suburban contexts. The incorporation of narrative elements and storyness into biblical preaching and teaching is a unique element that happens to be effective in all three types of areas.

The incorporation of narrative elements into preaching and teaching is not merely an issue of practicality and methodological effectiveness though. It is also deeply biblical. In many of the recorded sermons in Scripture, we find storyness used in both urban and rural contexts.

various types of storyness
in urban-set sermons

The book of Acts records a variety of these sermons from men like Peter,[5] Stephen,[6] Philip,[7] and Paul.[8] In many of these sermons, a variety of narrative elements are employed by the preacher in order to more powerfully and faithfully show the gospel, rather than simply tell it. The elements themselves vary, but in their variance they all reflect the importance of storyness for enhancing a sermon. Here are just a few of those sermons.

acts 4:8-12

In this brief sermon, Peter and John respond to questioning by the Jewish Sanhedrin about speaking boldly about Christ and the saving nature of the gospel. The Sanhedrin was the Jewish high court of justice, consisting of seventy-one men and led by the high priest. The council could decide almost any fate— except the death penalty, which was decided by the Romans. It was located in Jerusalem within the Chamber of the Hewn Stone inside Herod's temple and therefore at the center of Jerusalem's urban life.[9] Thus, the audience to which Peter and John were speaking was none other than the city's elites. It would be like speaking in Boston's Faneuil Hall in the nineteenth century or on the campus of Harvard University today. It was to these urbanites that the apostles proclaimed a gospel message of salvation through Christ alone.[10]

However, rather than merely stating that salvation is found in none other than Jesus, Peter employed narrative elements like literary imagery to show such is the case. In verse 11, he stated, "[Jesus] is the stone which was rejected by you, the builders, but which became the chief corner stone" (Acts 4:11 NASB). The statement is a quote from Psalm 118:22. Such a quote would have done two things for the listening audience. First, it would have directed the minds of the Jewish audience back to the familiar Old Testament Scriptures. Second, it would have crafted a verbal picture in their minds that illustrated the central thrust of the apostle's message. After all, it's one thing to say, "Jesus is the foundation of our salvation." It is quite another thing to show that he is such by using architectural imagery and familiar references. The latter is much more powerful!

acts 7:1–53

Like Peter, Stephen also used storyness in an urban-set sermon. When responding to the Sanhedrin's accusation of blasphemy, Stephen employed the element of historical narrative to validate his innocence. Just as Peter and John were forced to speak before the urban, religious elites of Jerusalem, Stephen was faced with a similar predicament. However, this time Stephen would need to use more than just literary imagery if he was going to both draw the Sanhedrin into a convincing retelling of the gospel and show that he was not a blasphemous heretic. Like an expert defense attorney, using the element of historical narrative, Stephen recounted the redemptive story of the gospel to show his audience both the truth of the gospel and the validity of his innocence. Commentator Andrew Knowles states:

> To explain his faith in Jesus, Stephen reviews the history of God's people (7:1–53). His hearers know the Old Testament story well, but Stephen has something new to show them. He reminds the Council of four heroes of faith: Abraham who never owned any land; Joseph who was exiled in Egypt; Moses who wandered the wilderness; and David who planned the temple. Gradually, Stephen's point becomes clear. God isn't restricted to any place or building. He is a pilgrim God who lives with his people—wherever they are. The temple is a meeting place for God and human beings. But now it is replaced by Jesus the Messiah. But the Jewish leaders have killed him! They claim to uphold the law, but they break it. They claim to serve God, but they persecute his prophets.[11]

Rather than simply stating that the gospel was true and he was innocent, Stephen showed his audience both by simply and effectively employing storyness. This is the power of integrating narrative into our witness and teaching!

acts 17:22–34

Acts 17:22–34 also records the use of narrative elements in an urban context, but this time by the apostle Paul. Here, Paul spoke rather philosophically to the people of Athens at the Areopagus. *Areopagus* means "hill of Mars," and it referred both to a hill in Athens (a Greek city and one of the most prominent urban centers in the Greco-Roman world) and to the Athenian council or court that met there. It was a world famous forum of debate and trial. Some five centuries before Paul's time, Socrates faced those who accused him of deprecating the Greek gods. By Paul's day, though, the council of the Areopagus was responsible for various political, educational, philosophical, and religious matters, as well as for legal proceedings. It was in this urban center of power that Paul was invited to speak after having reasoned with Jews and God-fearing Gentiles in the Athenian synagogue and marketplace several days earlier (Acts 17:16–21).[12]

While before the council, Paul was given the opportunity to proclaim the gospel. But rather than simply telling it by means of citing Old Testament passages that would have been unfamiliar to his pagan Greek audience, he instead showed it through an intellectual philosopher's approach.[13] For example in verse 24, Paul made the point that as creator God is bigger than we make him out to be, and as such, he is not a God who can be confined to a box or formula. To cement his point in the minds of his audience, Paul used a verbal picture. He said, the "Lord of heaven and earth, does not live in temples made by man" (Acts 17:24 ESV). Similarly, in verse 26, Paul made the point that God is sovereign. But instead of merely stating such, Paul showed it with his statement, "And he made from one man every nation of mankind to live on all the face of the earth, having determined allotted periods and the boundaries of their dwelling place" (ESV). The difference is that in directly citing a verse like Deuteronomy 32:8, which is itself a verbal picture of God's sovereignty, Paul was able to show and tell his point.

acts 20:17–35; 22:1–21; 26:1–23

This final example is most appropriate because it is an urban-set sermon that uses narrative elements to story the gospel. More precisely, it is a set of passages that records a farewell speech by Paul at Miletus to the elders visiting from the church of Ephesus; a defense of his mission to a crowd of Jews in Jerusalem; and later a defense of himself before King Agrippa and Queen

Bernice in Caesarea. In each of these passages though, the apostle Paul used the narrative element of personal testimony to show and tell his points. In other words, Paul made his specific point not merely with explanatory statements like "I know," "I believe," and "I heard," but with narrative statements like "I have experienced!"

In Acts 20:17–35, Paul defended himself, stating that as an apostle, his ministry had been one of not shrinking "from declaring to you anything that was profitable, and teaching you in public," but "testifying both to Jews and to Greeks of repentance toward God and faith in our Lord Jesus Christ" and not considering his life "of any value nor as precious to [himself], if only [he would] finish [his] course and the ministry that [he] received from the Lord Jesus, to testify to the gospel of the grace of God" (Acts 20:20–21, 24 ESV).

Later, in Acts 22:1–21, Paul again defended himself by stating, "Brothers and fathers, hear the defense that I now make before you" (22:1 ESV). He continued by sharing how he was born a Jew in Tarsus of Cilicia, and "persecuted this Way to the death, binding and delivering to prison both men and women," until he encountered Jesus on the road to Damascus (22:4 ESV).

Finally, in Acts 26:1–23, Paul presented a final defense: "I consider myself fortunate that it is before you, King Agrippa, I am going to make my defense today" (26:2 ESV). He continued by stating that he was raised and lived as a Pharisee according to the strictest sect of his religion and did many things hostile to the name of Jesus of Nazareth, until he was transformed by Jesus on the Damascus road (26:5, 9–18).

In each of these accounts, the preaching principle is clear. Paul did not settle for merely explaining the gospel or his innocence. Rather, he incorporated his personal testimony or story both to validate the gospel and to show his innocence. As such, his various defenses were no less logical and certainly more compelling for the first-century urbanites to whom he was speaking. Storyness made Paul's messages more faithful, convincing, and powerful for his urbanite audiences.

storyness in rural-set sermons

Earlier I mentioned that we can find storyness as a central component in sermons throughout the Bible, no matter if those sermons were delivered to urban or rural audiences. Having covered urban-set sermons, we now turn to those of a more rural context. Unfortunately, however, there are few, given the Bible's urban trajectory whereby creation starts in a garden in Genesis 1 and ends in a heavenly city in Revelation 21. Commentators Ryken, Wilhoit, and Longman describe the urban trajectory of the New Testament: "It is easy to see that the mission strategy of the early church was to evangelize the city. It is no exaggeration to say that in Acts the church is almost exclusively associated with the city, within which [to be sure] it is a tiny and persecuted minority. The picture of the city as church site is reinforced by the letters to the seven churches in Revelation 2–3."[14]

The implication here is that as the city went, so went the country. And as the city was won for Christ through the preaching and teaching of the gospel, so was the countryside also won. Consequently, and when it came to preaching, those aspects that were successful in urban contexts proved to be just as successful in rural contexts. This is after all, why the Greek word *paganos*, meaning "country dweller," is the word from which we get our English word *pagan*. It came to be used for those outside the city who had not yet heard the gospel but would soon be reached as the city and edges of the city began to be reached.

By way of conclusion then—because Christianity and the preaching and teaching of the Christian gospel was largely a movement from an urban setting outward to rural settings—we have reason to believe, even in the absence of direct record, that many of the preaching aspects that were effective for an urban audience were similarly effective for a rural audience, especially aspects like storyness that are more universal or "urbal" than not. From my own experience back in the rural settings of South Carolina and my two most recent preaching assignments, Salem Church near Saxapahaw and new**hope** in central North Carolina, there is no doubt in my mind that the power and effectiveness of narrative elements is both wise and applicable, regardless of an urban or rural setting.

What about contexts with far more disparity than urban versus rural? What about contexts that differ in terms of cultures, nationalities, and time periods, such as trying to read and preach a book written two thousand years ago? How do we bridge the gaps of that kind of wide-ranging context? As we start to bring closure to this book, let's take a hard look at contextualization and the role of narrative therein. As we will see, once again, it is the relevance and power of narrative that has the undeniable ability to connect us with people everywhere so that we can ultimately connect them with Christ.

the power of
narrative to
bridge the gaps

9

In 2010 our church embarked on a mission trip to Kiria, Kenya, with a wonderful organization called 410 Bridge. For most of us on the trip, this was our first time in Africa. As such, we had participated in all of the orientation workshops, received appropriate shots and vaccinations, and rallied prayer and financial support.

After several long flights, we loaded into buses and headed north to the remote village of Kiria. Despite all of our preparations, we were by no means prepared to encounter the breathtaking beauty of Africa and the Kenyan people.

My daughter Anna Grace and I had worked hard to memorize certain words so that we could connect on a deeper level with our brothers and sisters in Kenya. Everything was unfolding nicely until two or three days into our trip, while riding on the bus back toward our adopted village, I looked down the road and saw dozens of children playing. By this point, the bus was lively with enthusiasm and relationship building and everyone was getting along nicely. As I looked out of the window, I said the first thing that came to my mind. "Hey everyone, look at those kids." Most of the Americans on the bus simply followed the instruction, looked at the kids, and made comments about their joy and enthusiasm. However, I noticed that the few Kenyans around me looked confused and grew strangely silent. It wasn't until we stopped the bus some thirty miles later that our 410 Mission guide, by the name of Muchi, pulled me aside to say, "Here in Kenya, we actually refer to our dogs as 'kids.'" He went on to gently suggest that I not refer to their children as kids anymore. It was a humbling lesson for me in the importance of contextualization.

As preachers of the most important news on the planet, it is imperative that we fully grasp the nuances and importance of context. If we are not aware of how a given cultural context influences a certain situation, then we run the risk of reacting in a way that is contrary to the cultural context and rendering ourselves ineffective in communicating the gospel in that setting. Likewise, if we do not understand that context plays a huge role in how we understand and communicate Scripture, we will be unfaithful to the Bible and ineffective in communicating it to those around us. Being both faithful and effective in preaching biblical truth entails understanding and employing the idea of contextualization.

What do we mean by contextualization, and why is it important in a discussion about preaching with narrative elements? Simply speaking, when we refer to context, we are really talking about culture. When it comes to biblical preaching, it refers more specifically to the theological culture or heritage from which we or an audience comes.[1] For example, this might take the form of a theological preaching culture that elevates a more expository or verse-by-verse preaching style, bent on bringing great depth and knowledge of the Bible to hearers. For others, the theological preaching culture might take the form of a topical or more engagement-oriented method that seeks to make the principles and topics of the Bible interesting and compelling to hearers in order to engender faith. And, still for others of us as it was for me at Duke Divinity School, we might find ourselves in a context that highly values the power of narrative plot in the preaching experience. Regardless of the culture to which we are accustomed and which has shaped us, we have to admit that it is a limited one. For better or worse, our context is one among many, which means that it is by definition only one angle of a more diverse and greater social, cultural, and theological context.

Let's move from theory to the practical. Take, for example, a reading of Ephesians 5.[2] The apostle Paul stated, "Wives, submit to your own husbands, as to the Lord. For the husband is the head of the wife even as Christ is the head of the church, his body, and is himself its Savior. . . . Husbands, love your wives, as Christ loved the church and gave himself up for her, that he might sanctify her, having cleansed her by the washing of water with the word, so that he might present the church to himself in splendor, without spot or wrinkle or any such thing, that she might be holy and without blemish" (5:22–23, 25–27 ESV).

Wives, you know that reading this passage will look much different for you on a morning after having a late-night fight with your husband than it would after a great date, consisting of a surprise candlelight dinner at your favorite restaurant. Submission might at times seem to translate into being trampled on and miserable as opposed to the joyful giving of yourself to a loving husband. Likewise husbands, you know that reading this passage after learning of infidelity committed by your wife is going to take on a totally different feeling and application than it would on the first night of your honeymoon. The reason is that our context affects how we read Scripture. Likewise, it affects how we preach that Scripture as well. To neglect the influence that context exerts, therefore, is to be incredibly myopic, and ultimately unfaithful and ineffective in our teaching ministries. It is, for example, to tell a wife in your congregation to blindly submit to her husband without knowing that she has just discovered his affair. Neglecting context is biblically and practically unfaithful.

Again, for example, preaching about the power of Jesus who frees captives ought to look totally different when preached to a group of poor, Kenyan Christians who have battled through famine and persecution for the majority of their lives than it would to middle- or upper-class Americans, blessed with nice cars and insulated roofs over their heads. In the same way, preaching Luke 16:10–13 about not serving and idolizing money ought to look different for the American who has money and must consider the implications of generosity, stewardship, and the like than it would to the Haitian, who has very little money with which to be generous. Our context, both culturally and theologically, exerts great influence on how we read and communicate biblical truth. It must be taken into account.

wait a second here . . . are you saying . . . ?

I know what you might be thinking: "The idea of context affecting the way we read and communicate biblical truth scares the dickens out of us! It seems to imply that arbitrary and ever-changing cultural fads or experiences have the right to determine the meaning of the Bible. As Bible-believing preachers, we fiercely hold to the doctrine of *sola scriptura*, that final authority rests with the Bible. After all, if subjective experience can determine the meaning of the Bible, then we will find ourselves in a revolving door of relativism, which chops the authoritative legs of the Bible off at the knees." This is the precisely the kind of destructive relativism addressed in chapter 2.

Such a concern is completely legitimate and therefore makes it necessary that we ground our understanding of contextualization in four foundational principle.[3] First, passages like 2 Timothy 3:14–17 make it clear that the Bible is itself aware of the issue of context. It understands that it is God's message for people of *all* contexts and *all* generations, even when it was itself written in a specific context! Second Timothy 3:14–17 states, "But as for you, continue in what you have learned and have firmly believed, knowing from whom you learned it and how from childhood you have been acquainted with the sacred writings, which are able to make you wise for salvation through faith in Christ Jesus. All Scripture is breathed out by God and profitable for teaching, for reproof, for correction, and for training in righteousness, that the man of God may be complete, equipped for every good work" (ESV).

As we know, the Old and New Testaments were written and given to specific groups of readers with specific experiences, traditions, expectations, and contexts. For example, the Old Testament was given specifically to the nation of Israel, while the New Testament was given specifically to individual churches like the church at Galatia or Corinth through men like the apostle Paul. Yet the Bible tells us that it is still relevant for every issue and situation in the life of a modern hearer. This means that it fundamentally affirms the idea of contextualization without steeping into relativism. Consequently, as students and communicators of the Bible, we can and should feel free to speak biblical truth into various contexts without feeling as if we are being disingenuous to its overall truth.

Second, an interesting phenomenon that illuminates our understanding of contextualization occurs throughout the pages of the Bible: God often takes what was known in a given culture and fills it with new meaning. After all, isn't that at the heart of the meaning of Jesus' words about pouring new wine into old wineskins (Matt. 9:14–17)? Most scholars contend that Jesus was making a connection between his teaching and traditional Judaism. According to most reputable scholars, Jesus was pitting his new way of teaching against that of the Pharisees and scribes. Jesus did this all the time in the Gospels as he tried to enlighten the religious leaders that God was ushering in a new context and that the kingdom was bursting out among them. In other words, God has this proclivity for addressing specific contexts or issues, and then redefining those in order to communicate his purposes. Essentially, the Bible presents God as the world's first non-relativistic contextualizer!

For example, the Hebrew word *El* meaning "God" did not originate within Israelite culture though it was present in the Old Testament. Rather, prior to Israel's use of it, it was used to describe the false, Cannanite god Baal. But God took the word and applied it to himself as a term that Israel was to use for describing him. In other words, God took that which was already present and known within a particular context and reshaped it for his purposes.

The same can be said for the concept of the afterlife, which was present in Egyptian culture long before Israelite culture. But the Egyptian notion of the afterlife was radically different from the Judeo-Christian notion. The distinction came by means of God taking a concept that was familiar yet foreign to Israel, retranslating it, and filling it with new meaning so that Israel was not only able to understand it, but make it her own. Knowing that God is himself a non-relativistic contextualizer provides us with both the motivation and example by which to do the same when we communicate biblical truth.

A third principle of contextualization is that we can have adequate understanding of Scripture without necessarily having an exhaustive understanding. In other words, just because our own contexts are limited, it does not mean we are incapable of understanding overarching truths. Just as we do not need to know everything taking place in the mind of a friend at the time he or she writes us a letter in order to grasp the central meaning of the letter, so we do not have to grasp everything in the mind and context of biblical writers in order to grasp their central messages.

Take King David for example. Here was a man who had accurate insight about the Messiah who was to come, so much so that God called him "a man after his own heart" (1 Sam. 13:14; see also Acts 13:22) for his faith in the coming Christ. However, because Christ would not be born for another thousand years or so after David's life, David certainly did not and could not have had an exhaustive understanding about Jesus. Yet his lack of full understanding did not negate the ability for an accurate understanding.

David's ignorance did not prevent him from knowing the lay of the land. His limited context did not negate accurate understanding. Likewise, to acknowledge our context when it comes to communicating biblical truth is not a concession toward a lack of understanding. Rather, it is an acknowledgement of limitation that often fosters deeper understanding.

The final contextualization principle is that the Bible is the primary basis for our understanding of other parts of itself. In other words, although all expressions of Scripture are rooted in a specific context (a certain time, space, place, audience, etc.) and can be better understood by more fully understanding that context, it is the breath of Scripture that serves as the truest interpretive lens for any element of Scripture. That is, the internal coherence of Scripture allows us to interpret passages through the lens of other passages. This means that Scripture is best understood not so much in a specific cultural context or historical background but in the context of other Scripture. In other words, Scripture is the best interpreter of Scripture. Such a realization allows the biblical communicator to keep from over- or under-contextualizing and thereby rendering him- or herself unfaithful or ineffective as a communicator of the gospel.

In light of these foundational principles, contextualization is simply taking into consideration the cultural context from which the gospel comes and into which we are seeking to communicate.[4] It is, as one missions strategist defines, "the word we use for the process of making the gospel and the church as much at home as possible in a given cultural context."[5] And isn't this our fundamental job as Bible preachers and teachers anyway? To understand and translate scriptural truth into the language of our hearers has always been the task of the preacher. Contextualization helps us do just that, and in doing so, we become all the more faithful to Scripture and effective in communicating that truth to those around us.

the power of narrative to bridge the gaps

Dallas Theological Seminary professor of world missions and intercultural studies, Dr. Steve Strauss, says that all languages share common features, such as the use of stories, comparisons, contrasts, examples, and the articulation of feelings and emotions, just to name a few.[6] As such, all people are to some degree able to understand and relate to the culture and experiences of another.

In 2005 Amy Lynn and I decided to travel to London and Paris for our ten-year anniversary. After all, in those ten short years, she had delivered five amazing children, I had finished two master's degrees and my doctoral studies, and together we had given birth to new**hope** church. It had been an incredibly busy ten years, so we concluded it was okay to splurge a little and do it up right to celebrate! I am glad we did because this time away was nothing less than wonderful and the trip of a lifetime. Everything was lovely and delightful, with the exception of driving on the left side of the road. I knew that I was going to carry the full burden of this cultural difference when Amy Lynn took one look at the roads and rental car, handed me the keys, and walked to other side of the car. The driving was my responsibility. Thankfully, I stayed focused and we survived. Looking back on it though, it is safe to say that we hit the cities and the countryside in more ways than one!

Now, if we think that scenario through a little more, we can get a little more mileage out of the story. Just as it is difficult for this American to drive on the left side of the road, it is peculiarly difficult for a Brit to drive on the right side of the road. But that doesn't change the fact that we both share the common experience of driving, even though it looks slightly different depending on whose homeland we're driving in. In that sense, even though our preferred context of driving is different, we can totally relate.

The same applies for communicating and understanding biblical truth. A Westerner who has grown up in a free, democratic society may not be able to articulate the emotion of a passage like Acts 7 that describes the persecution and subsequent martyrdom of the apostle Stephen, as acutely as an Easterner who has grown up in an oppressive, communistic society. But because we all understand suffering to some degree, we can each relate to what it might have been like for Stephen to have been martyred.

The incorporation of narrative elements into our biblical communication does two things: First, it allows the communicator to bridge the inherent cultural and linguistic gaps amongst those of different contexts; gaps like those between an American and Asian, an Easterner and Westerner. A story gives a platform from which to communicate elements like comparison and contrast, emotion, and example which are universal to us all. Within a story, a communicator is able to illustrate, communicate feeling, draw parallels, and generally just speak in a manner that is understandable, even amongst different contexts. He or she is able to bridge contextual gaps in a way not otherwise possible through mere explanation or exemplification. Consequently, the communicator becomes all the more effective in his or her communication of biblical truth.

Second, the incorporation of narrative elements into our biblical communication allows us to not only be more effective, but also to be more scripturally faithful. As we utilize storyness, we model the inherent nature of Scripture as a grand, redemptive story centering on the person and work of Jesus Christ. As many have said, the Bible is the story of the anticipation (the Old Testament), manifestation (the four Gospels), proclamation (the book of Acts), explanation (the Epistles), and consummation (the book of Revelation) of Jesus Christ as the only name under heaven by which men and women are saved (Acts 4:12).

Jeannine K. Brown, in her book *Scripture as Communication*, summarizes the nature of the Bible like this: "Scripture is, at heart, communication."[7] In other words, the Bible is one big story intended to communicate to all people, of all generations and contexts that a king is returning. This means that the Bible is a sixty-six-book, 1,189-chapter, 31,103-verse story about the person and work of Jesus Christ, who serves as the foundation for humanity past, present, and future. To incorporate storyness into our communication of the Bible is therefore to model the nature of the Bible itself.

Our church just concluded a message series titled "At the Movies." In this series, we looked at one blockbuster movie each Sunday for a period of four weeks. The movies that we chose for this series were *Iron Man*, *Toy Story*, *Avatar*, and *The Blind Side*.

During the series, I particularly enjoyed the contextualization I had to think through in order to connect *Avatar* with our particular community of faith. The story is about the transformation of Jake Sully, an ex-marine, who lost the use of his legs due to war. Jake proudly wore the honor of being a marine by his words and attitude.

Jake's twin brother was a scientist, contracted to learn the ways of the Na'vi people on the planet Pandora. When Jake's brother was suddenly killed, Jake was asked to become his brother's avatar, to actually be placed inside the body of a replica Na'vi.

As an ex-marine, Jake couldn't stand the fact that he no longer had use of his legs. Becoming his brother's avatar gave him the chance to walk and run again. The avatar gave him the opportunity to begin again. If you saw and remember the movie, Jake was on assignment so he could move the Na'vi people off Pandora so the humans could extrapolate a valuable rock resource worth billions of dollars. However, the movie takes a sharp turn when Jake meets Neyteri, befriends the Na'vi people, and decides that they are the ones he is willing to fight for.

After showing one of the most violent fight scenes at the end of the film, I proclaimed this message:

Who will we fight for, new**hope**? What's worth fighting for? Can you imagine central North Carolina, if we, as a community of faith would fight for the hostiles. [That was the language of the movie and what the

Na'vi people were commonly called by the humans.]
Jake had to answer the question: For whom do you work
and live? The way he fights answers the question. The
way we live our lives answers the question for us, as
well. Our vision to reach, teach, and release is all about
fighting for what is right! We might get some things
wrong along the way, new**hope**, but we will fight for
what is right. We will fight for those who are lost and
facing a Christless eternity! We will fight even for those
who are most hostile to the message of grace! . . . We will
do anything short of sin to fight for those not yet in the
family of God! The overarching story of the Bible is
about God and God's people fighting for what is right in
order to get as many people as possible in the kingdom of
light so that together, we can push back the darkness! So,
just as Jake and the Na'vi people found themselves
engaged in a battle to death, we, too, are called by God
to fight till our last living breath to save those who don't
know Jesus. Listen church, there is a war waging every
day that we exist on this Pandora planet known as Earth,
and God is calling us to put on the full armor of God and
fight [Eph. 6:10–20]. As this planet continues to spin out
of control, make no mistake about it, kingdoms are clash-
ing! The question that *Avatar* thrusts our way today is
this: For whom will you fight?

What was I doing in this message? Basically, I was using a relevant story, drawn from the first billion-dollar movie in the history of humanity, and therein integrating the larger story of God and his people engaged in a battle over the eternal destiny of people's souls. I believe this is an appropriate example of how we can take the power of story and bridge the gaps between two differing contexts. Through the use of narrative, I was able to bridge the gap between the ancient meta-narrative of God's Word and a culturally relevant blockbuster that really had nothing to do with Christianity or the Bible. However, such is the power of story to bridge the gaps of contextualization and hopefully empower the body of Christ to fight for God's goodness in the world!

When we preach like this, we are truly emulating our Lord and Savior, Jesus Christ. The best storyteller of all time used narrative elements to not only connect with the first-century Palestinian crowds that were flocking to him, but I believe he did so because it is in story that we tap into a timeless form of communication that will continue to connect in multiple contexts for years and even centuries to come.

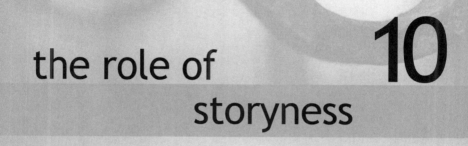

the role of

storyness

Hopefully, by now, I have convinced you of the importance, effectiveness, and faithfulness of incorporating narrative elements into your preaching, regardless of what style you are using on a given Sunday. As I remain a lifelong student of the Scriptures and continue with the weekly and audacious task of preaching the gospel, it has become crystal clear to me that my impact as a preacher is inextricably linked to my ability to become a master storyteller. No doubt, I have a long way to go, but this is an endeavor to which I am committed.

The incorporation of storyness and narrative elements into our preaching and teaching is not a stylistic or aesthetic issue. If it were, it would enhance our preaching and teaching in some contexts and diminish it in others. It would be like a particular style of fashion that is considered trendy in some places but ridiculous and hideous in others. But as we have seen, storyness is a feature that can enhance a sermon in a variety of settings, whether they are urban or rural or an eclectic combination of various contexts. Again, no one has been better at the art of communication than Jesus. Haddon Robinson, in making this connection to Jesus' teaching, put it like this:

> When Jesus appeared, He came telling stories, and most of them have entered the world's folklore. In fact, so brilliant a storyteller was Jesus that we sometimes miss the profound theology disguised in His tales of a rebellious delinquent and his insufferable brother, a pious Pharisee and a repentant tax collector, buried treasures, and a merchant who had an unexpected appointment with death. Narrative preaching however does not merely repeat a story as one would recount a pointless, worn-out joke. . . . In a narrative sermon, as in any other sermon, a major idea continues to be supported by other ideas, but the content supporting the points is drawn directly from the incidents in the story. . . . Narratives are most effective when the audience hears the story and arrives at the speaker's ideas without the ideas being stated directly.[1]

This is all about showing rather than telling. It is about helping people not only hear about the beauty of the gospel, but behold its beauty as much as possible. It is when we actually start to behold the good news of Jesus that we find ourselves captivated and ultimately transformed into the likeness of Christ. Second Corinthians 3:18 says it best: "And we, who with unveiled faces all reflect the Lord's glory, are being transformed into his likeness with ever-increasing glory, which comes from the Lord, who is the Spirit."

As we surveyed the landscape of Christian preaching, we found that the three preaching "crops" I discussed earlier—expository, topical, and narrative—have not only been prevalent at different times and places, but have all been used by God to effectively and faithfully proclaim the gospel and further advance God's kingdom. Furthermore, as history has produced a plethora of successful preachers and teachers all employing these various styles, it becomes apparent that expository, topical, and narrative sermons can be equally faithful to Scripture and relevant for communicating to our twenty-first-century culture. This means we can be free to handle God's Word in many different ways depending on our ministry context, so long as we continue to preach the beauty of the gospel with Jesus as the heart-captivating hero as opposed to merely our example, educator, life coach, therapist, or the like.

I liken this freedom to use different preaching styles to the sport of golf. I know that some of you would dispute whether or not golf is a sport, but stick with me. Any good golfer, of which I am not, will tell you that in order to play a good round of eighteen holes you need to use every golf club in your bag.

Can you imagine someone trying to play a round of golf with only a putter or driver? Any good golfer knows that he or she has to use all the tools in the golf bag. In the same way, I believe it is wise for preachers to feel comfortable using the various sermon styles that we have in our preaching bag.

Maybe it's because of my experience of being exposed to the three predominant preaching styles in my early years of ministry, but I choose to use different styles of messages regularly. It is not uncommon for me to preach an expository sermon series as I am doing right now. As I write this closing chapter, I need to work on my first message in a series called "Colossians—a Robust Discipleship." Over the course of the next four weeks, I will methodically walk the congregation through each of the four chapters in a somewhat verse-by-verse fashion. Last month, as I have already said, I led the church through a topical series titled "At the Movies," where we used clips from four blockbuster movies and extrapolated topics that struck a chord with our culture. I used the Scriptures to enlighten those topics with a biblical worldview. With Christmas right around the corner, I will preach a narrative series titled "A Simple Christmas." The story of Emmanuel, God with us, preached and foretold by the prophets and coming with the birth of baby Jesus as the Messiah of the world, lends itself perfectly to the power of plot and narrative. So, in a period of four months, I will actually use three different styles of preaching.

As you can see, I am not arguing for a particular style of preaching. Let me be as clear as possible. What I am vigorously arguing for is not to lock into one style or another, but that regardless of the style or styles you like to preach, make it a habit to always integrate narrative elements into every sermon. Maybe you are in a setting where expository verse-by-verse preaching is best and most compatible with the preaching diet of your people. Or maybe you are in a highly academic setting and it is precisely the power of narrative that most engages the people. Or maybe you are in a setting where the needs of that particular community warrant topical preaching. Regardless, what I am suggesting is that the integration of narrative elements—the power of God's meta-narrative linking all of humanity's smaller stories together—will help your preaching become more effective in seeing people come to Christ and maturing fully devoted disciples.

What storyness adds to expository, topical, and narrative sermons is the ability to illuminate the gospel in a more profound and personal way. Narrative elements do more than just tell us that Jesus is the hero; they show us. They allow us to behold rather than just hear about the beauty of the gospel.

As the preacher "stories" the beauty of the gospel, we not only give ourselves a greater possibility for penetrating the minds of our hearers, but their hearts as well. And the degree to which our hearts are penetrated by the gospel, as a tree is penetrated by water, is the degree to which our lives will be transformed from the inside out, as a tree is pushed to grow from the roots up.

The Reformer Martin Luther said it best: "Now preaching ought to have the object of promoting faith in [Jesus]."[2] The use of narrative elements or storyness in our communication of the gospel gives us the best possible opportunity for promoting that faith in Christ. Narrative elements show rather than simply tell of the captivating beauty of the gospel, which when beheld in our hearts and minds, naturally culminate in faith and worship toward our Creator. After all, God's Word never returns void after penetrating a heart (Isa. 55:11). The question becomes: Will we preach and present the gospel with the use of narrative elements, so that it can do its penetrating work?

Growing up, I occasionally started my Saturday mornings, as every good 1970s and 1980s child did, with a little TV. I would start with my favorite cartoons with characters such as Bugs Bunny, Fat Albert, Spider Man, and Mickey Mouse. But my dad often came in and changed the channel. (This must be a universal prerequisite to being a father, because I find myself doing the same today.) At first, this change of the channel would bother me, but I vividly remember us landing on a television show being hosted by an artist named Bob Ross. To say I was captivated by the words and artwork of Bob Ross is an understatement, to say the least.

If you remember, Bob Ross was the PBS, father-figure painter with the soothing voice and bushy beard. He managed to construct "happy little rivers and mountains" out of nothing on a blank canvas. What was so intriguing to me about this artist was how he painted. For thirty minutes straight, he would stand between the television camera and his canvas and tell the viewer what he was about to paint and how he was going to throw a streak of green paint here and dab it with a touch of brown there to form his iconic "happy little tree." The thing about Bob Ross, though, was that he never settled for simply telling you how to paint. Rather, he followed up his words of instruction with a picture of those words.

I remember listening to Mr. Ross describe how he was going to paint a mountain or forest scene and thinking, "That is never going to work. There is no way the beauty he is telling me about is actually going to manifest itself on that canvas." And then this talented artist would throw that streak of paint onto his canvas, leaving me stunned that in a matter of sheer moments he had brought to life a "happy little mountain range," teeming with life and beauty.

The most amazing thing about Bob Ross was that he could make a seemingly boring art show fascinating to a little kid like me. He did this, no doubt, by not just telling us about the beauty of art but by showing us! He allowed the viewer to behold his art's beauty through everything he said and did. In a sense, Bob Ross was the consummate communicator of the storyness of art. Had he not been, I am pretty sure that his show would have been on air for about two minutes. But as it was, Bob Ross painted on television for over ten years, until he passed away in 1995. Still to this day, when I come across a rerun of Bob Ross storytelling his happy art, I cannot help but stop the channel surfing, watch, experience, and enjoy the beauty of his work. Bob Ross left impressions of beauty in the minds and hearts of his viewers. And yet, with him, it was simply about oil paintings.

How much more, for us who possess the most inherently beautiful truth known to man, should we use our very best storytelling words to paint the best possible portrait of the gospel of Jesus Christ? As we integrate narrative elements and become master storytellers, I believe we will find that those who so graciously grant us the opportunity to speak—believers and nonbelievers alike—will be captivatingly engaged in our messages, converted to Christ, and growing as fully devoted followers of Jesus! In doing so, I believe we will be counted among those approved to preach this treasured gospel and who correctly handle the Word of truth (2 Tim. 2:15).

notes

Introduction

1. See, for example, Eugene L. Lowry, "The Revolution of Sermonic Shape," in *Listening to the Word: Studies in Honor of Fred B. Craddock*, eds. Gail R. O'Day and Thomas G. Long (Nashville: Abingdon, 1993), 93–112.

Chapter 2

1. American Dialect Society, "Truthiness," accessed December 5, 2011, http://www.americandialect.org/Word-of-the-Year_ 2006.pdf.
2. Alvin L. Reid, *Radically Unchurched: Who They Are & How to Reach Them* (Grand Rapids, Mich.: Kregel, 2002), 91.
3. *The New York Times*, "Hardcover Nonfiction," accessed December 5, 2011, http://www.nytimes.com/2006/01/29/books/bestseller/ 0129besthardnonfiction.html.
4. Brooks Egerton, "If God Himself Gave Freedom: Cardinal Arinze Says Force Has No Place in Faith Matters," *Dallas Morning News*, March 20, 1999.
5. Albert Mohler, "Ministry Is Stranger Than It Used to Be: The Challenge of Postmodernism" (blog), July 15, 2004, http://www.albertmohler.com/2004/07/15/ministry-is-stranger-than-it-used-to-be-the-challenge-of-postmodernism/.
6. A. W. Tozer, *The Knowledge of the Holy* (New York: Harper & Row, 1961), 1–2.

7. Fyodor Dostoyevsky, *The Brothers Karamazov* (New York: Bantam Dell, 2003).

Chapter 3

1. Robert Smith Jr., *Doctrine that Dances: Bringing Doctrinal Preaching and Teaching to Life* (Nashville: B&H, 2008), 75.
2. James F. Stitzinger, "The History of Expository Preaching," *The Master's Seminary Journal* 3, no. 1 (Spring 1992): 8, http://www.tms.edu/tmsj/tmsj3a.pdf.
3. John Albert Broadus, *Lectures on the History of Preaching* (New York: Sheldon, 1886), 7.
4. Stitzinger, 9.
5. Ibid., 10.
6. Ibid.
7. Lenny Luchetti, "Narrative Preaching," *Wesley Seminary at Indiana Wesleyan University* (seminary blog), August 23, 2010, http://wesleyanseminary.wordpress.com/2010/08/23/narrative-preaching-by-lenny-luchetti/.
8. Stitzinger, 11.
9. Kevin Craig, "Is the 'Sermon' Concept Biblical?" *Searching Together* 15 (Spring/Summer 1968): 25.
10. Ibid., 28.
11. Stitzinger, 14.
12. James Philip, "Preaching in History," *Evangelical Review of Theology* 8 (1984): 300.
13. Stitzinger, 16.
14. Ibid., 16–17.
15. John Calvin, *Institutes of the Christian Religion*, trans. and annotated Ford Lewis Battles (1536; repr., Grand Rapids, Mich.: Eerdmans, 1975), 195.
16. D. Martyn Lloyd-Jones, *The Puritans: Their Origins and Successors* (Edinburgh, U.K.: Banner of Truth, 1987), 375, 378.
17. Stitzinger, 24.
18. Benjamin Franklin, "The Great Awakening," accessed December 5, 2011, http://www.freewebs.com/firstgreatawakening/quotes.htm.
19. Stitzinger, 25, 27.

Chapter 4

1. Thomas G. Long, *The Witness of Preaching* (Louisville: Westminster John Knox, 1989), 25–26.

2. Karl Barth, *Homiletics* (Louisville: Westminster John Knox, 1991), 57.
3. William H. Willimon and Richard Lischer, *Concise Encyclopedia of Preaching* (Louisville: Westminster John Knox, 1995), 130–131.
4. Paul Borden, *Handbook of Expository Preaching: A Wealth of Counsel for Creative and Effective Proclamation* (Nashville: Broadman Press, 1992), 53–66.
5. Haddon Robinson, *Biblical Preaching: The Development and Delivery of Expository Messages* (Grand Rapids, Mich.: Baker, 2001), 21.
6. Yngve Brillioth, *A Brief History of Preaching* (Philadelphia: Fortress, 1945), 2.
7. Ibid., 5.
8. John R. W. Stott, *Between Two Worlds: The Challenge of Preaching Today* (Grand Rapids, Mich.: Eerdmans, 1982), 15.
9. John McClure, *Expository Preaching* (Louisville: Westminster John Knox, 1995), 132.
10. Ibid., 131.
11. Thomas Long, *The Witness of Preaching* (Louisville: Westminster John Knox, 1989), 20.
12. James Packer, "Preaching as Biblical Interpretation," *Inerrancy and Common Sense*, eds. Roger R. Nicole and J. Ramsey Michaels (Grand Rapids, Mich.: Baker, 1980), 41–54.
13. John MacArthur, *Rediscovering Expository Preaching* (Nashville: Thomas Nelson, 1992), 23.
14. Charles R. Swindoll, *Laugh Again: Experience Outrageous Joy* (Nashville: Thomas Nelson, 1992).
15. Ibid., "The Hidden Secret of a Happy Life," 75–90.
16. Ibid., "Freeing Yourself Up to Laugh Again," 189–208.
17. G. Campbell Morgan, *Sanctification* (New York: Revell, 1941).
18. Fred B. Craddock, *As One without Authority* (Nashville: Abingdon, 1971), 35.
19. W. M. Urban, *Language and Reality: The Philosophy of Language and the Principles of Symbolism* (London: Allen and Unwin, 1939), 49.
20. Amos Wilder, *Early Christian Rhetoric: The Language of the Gospel* (London: SCM, 1964), 26.

Chapter 5

1. J. Randall Nichols, *The Restoring Word: Preaching as Pastoral Communicator* (San Francisco: Harper, 1987), 16.
2. John R. W. Stott, *Between Two Worlds: The Challenge of Preaching Today* (Grand Rapids, Mich.: Eerdmans, 1982), 149.
3. Charles Jefferson, *The Minister as Shepherd: The Privileges and Responsibilities of Pastoral Leadership* (New York: Crowell, 1912), 95.
4. Ibid. (Fort Washington, Pa.: Christian Literature Crusade, 2006), 6.
5. Francis Rossow, "Topical Preaching," in *Handbook of Contemporary Preaching*, ed. Michael Duduit (Nashville: Broadman, 1992), 84.
6. James Cox, "Topical Preaching" in *Concise Encyclopedia of Preaching*, eds. William H. Willimon and Richard Lischer (Louisville: Westminster John Knox, 1995), 493.
7. Ibid.
8. Augustine, *On Christian Doctrine* (New York: Liberal Arts, 1958), 4.2.3.
9. Bill Hybels, "Real Men Don't Eat Quiche," *Preaching Today*, audiocassette, 2007.
10. Cox, 492–493.
11. Richard Caemmerer, *Preaching for the Church* (St. Louis, Mo.: Concordia, 1959), 139.
12. Rossow, 91.

Chapter 6

1. H. Grady Davis, *Design for Preaching* (Philadelphia: Fortress, 1958), 157.
2. Thomas Long, *The Witness of Preaching* (Louisville: Westminster John Knox, 1989), 36.
3. Simon Kistemaker, "Jesus as Story Teller: Literary Perspectives on the Parables," *The Master's Seminary Journal* 16, no. 1 (Spring 2005): 49, 55, http://www.tms.edu/tmsj/tmsj16b.pdf.
4. Eugene Lowry, *The Homiletical Plot: The Sermon as Narrative Art Form* (Louisville: Westminster John Knox, 2001), xix–xxi.
5. Ibid., 23.
6. David Buttrick, *Preaching Jesus Christ: An Exercise in Homiletic Theology* (Philadelphia: Fortress, 1988), 33.
7. Both sermons can be found in J. Ellsworth Kalas, *Old Testament Stories from the Backside* (Nashville: Abingdon, 1995).

8. Ibid., 16.
9. Ibid., 95.
10. Ibid., 98.
11. David Buttrick, *Homiletic Moves and Structures* (Philadelphia: Fortress, 1987), 12.
12. Roger Van Harn, *Pew Rights: For People Who Listen to Sermons* (Grand Rapids, Mich.: Eerdmans, 1992), 47.
13. Charles L. Campbell, *Preaching Jesus: The New Directions for Homiletics in Hans Frei's Postliberal Theology* (Grand Rapids, Mich.: Eerdmans, 1997), xi.
14. Fred Craddock, *Overhearing the Gospel*, rev. ed. (n.p.: Chalice Press, 2002), 45.
15. ———, *As One without Authority* (n.p.: Chalice Press, 2001), 49–50.
16. Paul Tillich, "You Are Accepted," *Preaching Today*, audiocassette, 1971.

Chapter 7

1. Richard Weaver, *Ideas Have Consequences* (Chicago: University of Chicago Press, 1948), 176.
2. Ibid., 58.
3. "Mental Health and Substance Abuse: Facts and Figures," World Health Organization, last modified August 18, 2006, http://www.searo.who.int/en/Section1174/Section1199/Section1567/Section1826_8101.htm.

Chapter 8

1. Percept, Close the Gap Demographics (1999).
2. Ibid.
3. Ibid.
4. Ibid.
5. Peter's sermons are recorded in Acts 2:14–41; 3:12–26; 4:8–12; 5:29–32; 10:35–49.
6. Stephen's sermon is recorded in Acts 7:2–53.
7. Philip's sermon is recorded in Acts 8:26–38.
8. Paul's sermons are recorded in Acts 16:30–34; 17:22–34; 19:1–7; 20:17–35; 22:1–21; 23:1–6; 24:10–21; 26:1–23; 28:23–28.
9. Logos Bible Software. Logos Bible Software Infographics (Bellingham, Wa.: Logos Bible Software, 2009).
10. Ted Cabal, ed., *The Apologetics Study Bible* (Nashville: Holman Bible Publishers, 2007), 1627.

11. Andrew Knowles, *The Bible Guide: An All-in-One Introduction to the Book of Books* (Minneapolis, Minn.: Augsburg, 2001), 543–544.

12. Walter A. Elwell and Barry J. Beitzel, *Baker Encyclopedia of the Bible* (Grand Rapids, Mich.: Baker, 1988), 167–168.

13. Lawrence O. Richards, *The Bible Readers Companion*, electronic ed. (Wheaton, Ill.: Victor, 1991), 724.

14. The idea of "City" in Leland Ryken, James C. Wilhoit, Tremper Longman III, eds., *Dictionary of Biblical Imagery* (Downers Grove, Ill.: InterVarsity, 1998).

Chapter 9

1. Steve Strauss, "Foundations for Contextualization: The Role of the Text" (lecture, Reformed Theological Seminary, Charlotte, N.C., 2007).

2. Ibid.

3. Ibid.

4. Juan Sanchez, "To Contextualize or Not to Contextualize: That Is NOT the Question," *The Gospel Coalition* (blog), December 13, 2009, http://thegospelcoalition.org/blogs/tgc/2009/12/13/to-contextualize-or-not-to-contextualize-that-is-not-the-question/.

5. "Putting Contextualization in Its Place," *9Marks* (Jul–Aug 2009), [accessed January 18, 2012,] http://www.9marks.org/ejournal/putting-contextualization-its-place.

6. Strauss.

7. Jeannine K. Brown, *Scripture as Communication: Introducing Biblical Hermeneutics* (Grand Rapids, Mich.: Baker Academic, 2007), 13.

Chapter 10

1. Haddon Robinson, *Biblical Preaching: The Development and Delivery of Expository Messages* (Grand Rapids, Mich.: Baker, 2001), 130.

2. Martin Luther, *Concerning Christian Liberty* (n. p.: CreateSpace, 2011), 18.